LAST SUPPER AND LORD'S SUPPER

The Didsbury Lectures

The Didsbury Lectures are delivered annually at the
British Isles Nazarene College, Manchester

The following series are available:

F. F. BRUCE, *Men and Movements in the Primitive Church*
T. TORRANCE, *The Mediation of Christ*
J. ATKINSON, *Martin Luther: Prophet to the Church Catholic*
C. K. BARRETT, *Church, Ministry & Sacraments in the
New Testament*
D. GUTHRIE, *Relevance of John's Apocalypse*
R. E. CLEMENTS, *Wisdom in Theology*
C. E. GUNTON, *Christ and Creation*

Forthcoming:
J. D. G. DUNN, *Christian Liberty*
M. HOOKER, *The Death of Christ*

LAST SUPPER AND LORD'S SUPPER

by

I. HOWARD MARSHALL

Professor of New Testament Exegesis,
University of Aberdeen

THE PATERNOSTER PRESS
Carlisle UK

British Library Cataloguing in Publication Data
Marshall, Ian Howard
  1. Lord's Supper—Biblical teaching
  I. Title
  232.9'   BV823

ISBN 0–85364–313–X

Typeset by Butler & Tanner, Frome, Somerset,
and Printed in Great Britain for The Paternoster Press,
P.O. Box 300, Carlisle, CA3 0QS, UK
by The Guernsey Press Co. Ltd., Guernsey, Channel Islands.

To
Archibald Macbride Hunter
teacher, colleague and friend

Contents

Preface

This book contains an expanded form of the series of Didsbury Lectures given at the British Isles Nazarene College, Manchester, in March, 1980. An earlier form of the lectures was given at the Summer School of Theology organized by St Mary's College in the University of St Andrews in June, 1978. I should like to take this opportunity of expressing my warm thanks to my friends in St Andrews and Manchester for their gracious hospitality and Christian fellowship during the delivery of the lectures.

For some time there has been a need for a simple but comprehensive survey of current study of the Last Supper and the Lord's Supper in the New Testament. There has been a considerable amount of recent work on the subject, and I cannot pretend to have mastered all of it; my aim has been simply to provide a general account of the topic which may serve as an introduction to the more detailed monographs on the subject. My treatment has been strictly confined to the New Testament, and I have said nothing about the history of the Lord's Supper during the following centuries, but my hope is that this book may contribute to a fresh understanding of the celebration of the Lord's Supper in the church today by reminding us of the New Testament basis of the sacrament.

I am grateful to my audiences at the lectures for their helpful comments, and also to my friends, the Rev. Daniel J. Antwi and Dr Colin J. Hemer, for their careful reading of the manuscript.

I. Howard Marshall
May, 1980

Abbreviations

CHAPTER ONE

Religious Meals in the Ancient World

It is arguable that the most important of the five senses for the Christian is the sense of hearing. In the opinion of the contributor to G. Kittel's *Theological Dictionary of the New Testament* on the word 'ear', 'The ear of the hearer is the most important organ for the proclamation of Jesus and hence for the process of faith.'[1] It would not be difficult to substantiate this statement from the New Testament. The message of Jesus was primarily a proclamation which reached the minds of people and so demanded a response from their wills through the sense of hearing. If in modern western civilisation the channel of communication is increasingly the eye which can read books and observe a TV screen, it still remains true that what God communicates to mankind is a message couched in words that calls for understanding and commitment.

Although, therefore, it is the Word of God which is the vehicle of the gospel, there is nevertheless a place for the other senses to be used in the communication of the gospel and in the expression of human response to it. The sense of smell is doubtless the least important of these; if some branches of the church use incense in their worship, this is meant to signify something that is sweet-smelling and thus acceptable to God rather than to appeal to the worshippers' sense of smell. The sense of touch is important in the rite of laying on of hands which is used in many branches of the church as a means of ordination or blessing; it is a means of expressing in a physical manner a spiritual action. There are, however, two actions in particular which call the senses into operation. In both cases the sense of hearing is involved and indeed may be said to be indispensable, but what is said is an accompaniment to, and an explanation of, an action which can be seen and in which the recipient is involved. The first of these actions is baptism which may be regarded as involving the senses of sight and touch: the person being baptised sees the water and feels it being applied to him. The second is the Lord's Supper which involves the senses of sight and taste, as the recipient sees the bread and wine and then participates of them. Baptism and the Lord's Supper convey the message of the gospel in a visible form, and at the same time they provide means by which the recipient can give outward, physical expression to his inward response to the message.

Within the Protestant churches these two actions have come to be known as sacraments, although the Roman Catholic Church and the Orthodox Church both reach a total of seven sacraments by including other rites such as confirmation and ordination. The Protestant churches argue that baptism and the Lord's Supper are the two actions which were specifically commanded by Jesus; the command to baptise forms part of the great commission to evangelise the world given by Jesus after his resurrection (Mt. 28:19), and the command to observe the Lord's Supper in memory of him forms part of the sayings uttered at his Last Supper with his disciples (Lk. 22:19; 1 Cor. 11:24f.).[2] The two commands are also of universal application, and they are linked together in a passage in 1 Corinthians where Paul is talking about their spiritual equivalents in the history of the people of Israel during their journey out of Egypt under Moses (1 Cor. 10:1–4).

Our concern in this book is with the second of these actions, the Lord's Supper, and our general aim will be to examine the teaching of the New Testament on this topic both for its own interest and also for its significance for our contemporary church life.

THE NEW TESTAMENT VOCABULARY

Our subject is known by a variety of names in the different

branches of the Protestant churches, and each of them can claim some basis in the New Testament.

Perhaps the most commonly used name is 'the Holy Communion', a term which is derived from Paul's statement in 1 Cor. 10:16: 'The cup of blessing which we bless, is it not a communion of the blood of Christ? The bread which we break, is it not a communion of the body of Christ?' (RV). Modern translations have rightly abandoned the use of the term 'communion' in this verse. They use such terms as 'participation' (RSV; NIV), 'sharing' (TEV), or 'means of sharing' (NEB) to bring out the meaning of the Greek word *koinōnia* more clearly, but they are not likely to drive the term 'communion' out of use as a designation for the sacrament.

A second term, which is also widely used, is 'the Lord's Supper'. This represents the actual term which Paul uses to describe the church's common meal in 1 Cor. 11:20 when he criticises the Corinthians for the way in which they are celebrating it and says, 'When you meet together, it is not the Lord's supper that you eat'. We may compare how he uses the same kind of language earlier when he speaks of Christians partaking of 'the table of the Lord' (1 Cor. 10:21). 'The Lord's Supper' is the term which is preferred in my own denomination, the Methodist Church, and I shall normally use it in what follows.

A third term, which is used especially by the Christian Brethren, is 'the Breaking of Bread'. Luke uses this term in Acts 2:42 (*cf.* Lk. 24:35) for what is in all probability the Lord's Supper, and the corresponding verbal form 'to break bread' is used by Paul when referring to the Lord's Supper in 1 Cor. 10:16 and also by Luke in Acts 2:46; 20:7, 11; 27:35.[3]

Finally, there is the term 'the Eucharist'. This word is derived from a Greek word which means 'thanksgiving' and is based on the giving of thanks that is an essential part of the Lord's Supper. The noun itself is not found in the New Testament, except as a variant textual reading in 1 Cor. 10:16, but the corresponding verb 'to give thanks' has a firm place in the biblical texts (Mk. 14:23; Lk. 22:17, 19; 1 Cor. 11:24). This term apparently became the favourite one in the early church (Did. 9:1, 5; Ign. Phld. 4; Smyr. 8:1), and it is the source for the adjective 'eucharistic' which is a useful addition to our theological vocabulary of technical terms.

These, then, are the biblically-based terms used to refer to this sacrament.[4] I have not included the term commonly used in the Roman Catholic Church, 'the Mass', since this word is not derived from biblical usage but comes from the use of the Latin term *missio* to refer to the dismissal, before the Lord's Supper was celebrated, of those who were not yet full members of the church.

A PRELIMINARY SURVEY OF THE SOURCES

When we turn to the New Testament to look for information about the Lord's Supper, we find that at first sight the evidence is extremely meagre. If Paul's first letter to the church at Corinth had not survived, and if that church had not needed to be admonished about the behaviour of some of its members at the meal, we should know next to nothing about how the meal was celebrated in the early church. 1 Corinthians 11:17–34 is the one biblical account of any length which discusses the actual conduct of the Lord's Supper in the church. It is not, of course, the only place where it is mentioned. There is a significant passage earlier in the same letter in connection with the question of whether Christians could eat food that had been offered in sacrifice to idols, and especially whether they might take part in meals in pagan temples (1 Cor. 10:1–22). There are the passages in Acts which refer to Christians breaking bread together, and in addition there are possible allusions to the meal in Hebrews 13:10–16; 1 Peter 2:3; 1 John 5:8; Jude 12 and Revelation 3:20. One or two passages have been thought to reflect liturgical formulae used in connection with the meal (1 Cor. 16:22; Rev. 22:17–21), and a number of passages refer to a form of church discipline which involved exclusion from the common church meal (1 Cor. 5:11; *cf.* 2 Thes. 3:6). 1 Corinthians 12:13b, however, is a reference to baptism and not to the Lord's Supper.

This short list of passages is fairly exhaustive so far as the Lord's Supper is concerned. Fortunately it is not the sum total of the evidence, for we also have a set of passages which describe the event which the early church regarded as the pattern for the Lord's Supper. The Last Supper held by Jesus with his disciples was understood to provide the model for the church's celebration of the Lord's Supper. Paul inserts a traditional account of what took place at it in the context of his own instructions to the church in Corinth (1 Cor. 11:23–26), and parallel accounts are to be found at the appropriate places in the three Synoptic Gospels (Mt. 26:17–30; Mk. 14:12–26; Lk. 22:7–38). It is important to remember that these accounts describe the *Last* Supper; they are therefore not direct witnesses for the procedure

followed at the *Lord's* Supper, although the way in which the
last meal of Jesus is described may well have been influenced by
the use of the narrative to provide a pattern for the church to
follow.

There is no corresponding account of the eating of bread and
the drinking of wine in the Gospel of John, although a supper
held by Jesus with his disciples on the eve of his death is
described in John 13. However, there are allusions to eating the
flesh and drinking the blood of Jesus in the discourse-material
which follows John's account of the feeding of the five thousand
(Jn. 6: especially 51–58), and in this connection we should
observe that the language in which the feeding miracles are
described in all four Gospels is sufficiently close to the language
used to describe the Last Supper as to raise the question whether
there is a deliberate parallelism.

We now have before us an inventory of the New Testament
material relating to our subject. There are several aims that we
may pursue as we examine it. Broadly speaking, we want to ask
a historical question, what actually happened at the Lord's
Supper? – and a theological question, what was the significance
of what happened? These two basic questions can each be divided
up into a number of subsidiary enquiries. Thus we need to know
something of the other sacred meals which were celebrated in the
ancient world, since these may well shed light on what happened
at the church's meal. There is also the extremely important
question of what actually happened at the Last Supper; there are
some differences between our sources, and we are faced by a
particularly tricky question in determining the course of events,
and how far the practice of the early church was determined by a
pattern given to it by Jesus. Then we must ask whether the
early church celebrated the Lord's Supper in the same way at
different times and places or whether there were differences in
practice. Finally, we want to know what theological interpretation was given to the Last Supper and the Lord's Supper, and
again whether there were differences in understanding the latter
in different parts of the church. All of this constitutes a formidable agenda, and it is not made any the easier by the way in
which the various aspects of the problem are closely intertwined.
A particular difficulty arises from the fact that many scholars are
sceptical whether the accounts of the Last Supper are historically
reliable in detail and would argue that our starting point ought to
be what the early church did rather than what Jesus did. Although
I do not share this scepticism, this does not enable me to avoid

the task of justifying my belief that we can learn what Jesus did
from the New Testament accounts.

Our procedure will be to start by considering the background
to the Last Supper and the Lord's Supper. Then we shall
examine the various accounts of the Last Supper to determine
their historical basis. This will then enable us to consider the
theological significance of the Last Supper. Finally, we shall
look at the Lord's Supper in the light of the Last Supper.

THE RELIGIOUS ASPECTS OF JEWISH MEALS

It is a golden rule of all interpretation that any action must be
seen in its historical setting and any text must be interpreted in
the light of its context, and therefore we must begin by looking
at the background to the meal which Jesus and his followers ate
together. In the ancient world, as everywhere else, people ate
meals primarily for the sake of satisfying their hunger and enjoying the pleasure given by food and drink. This point, obvious
as it may seem, perhaps needs to be stressed over against a
tendency one sometimes finds to suggest that other features were
uppermost. However, alongside this basic motive for eating
there were others.

In particular, a meal was often a social occasion to be enjoyed
in the company of other people and it could serve as an expression of hospitality, friendliness and unity. The reconciliation
between Jacob and Laban after the former's flight from Haran
was sealed by a sacrifice and a meal (Gn. 31:54). The connection
which we find in this particular example between the offering
of sacrifice and the holding of a meal was a common one. The
carcase of an animal which was offered to God in sacrifice could
be disposed of in various ways. In some cases the whole of the
animal was burnt either on the altar or outside the sanctuary,
but only part of a peace offering was burnt on the altar; the
rest of the animal was available for consumption by the offerer
along with his family and friends (Lv. 7:11–21). Since sacrifice
could be offered only in the one place appointed by God, the law
in Deuteronomy made provision for a non-sacrificial slaying of
animals for food in places that were distant from the sanctuary
(Dt. 12:15–28). But when the people of Israel came to the
sanctuary, offered an animal in sacrifice, and then shared in a
common meal, they could be said to be eating before the Lord,
and the occasion was one of praise and rejoicing (Dt. 12:7;
1 Ch. 29:21f.; 2 Ch. 7:7–10).[5] Since certain parts of the animal

eaten at such a meal had been offered in sacrifice to Yahweh, the meal could be regarded as an occasion of communion between him and his people. It should, however, be noted that there is no suggestion that Yahweh was thought of as eating the portion of the animal offered on the altar. As H. H. Rowley comments, 'If God were thought of as sharing the meal, we should expect him to have some of the best cuts'[6] rather than the blood and fat which were offered to him. Rather the people ate in the presence of God, a motif that is strikingly depicted in the story of how Moses and the elders went up the mountain and saw the God of Israel without being harmed by the experience: 'He did not lay his hand on the chief men of the people of Israel; they beheld God, and ate and drank' (Ex. 24:11). We should also observe that there is never any suggestion in the Old Testament that the worshippers ate the deity, although this idea is found in some other religions and may have been found in Babylonian religion (Je. 7:18; 44:19).[7]

At an ordinary Jewish meal, as distinct from the sacrificial meals which have just been discussed, the religious aspect was expressed by the giving of thanks to God at both the beginning and the end. The commencement of the meal was marked by the head of the household taking a piece of bread in his hands and saying a prayer of thanks over it: 'Blessed art thou, O Lord our God, King of the world, who bringest forth bread from the earth'. The bread was then broken into pieces and shared among all those present. It has been suggested that 'in this way every participant in the meal received a share of the benediction',[8] but this seems to be a mistaken notion since the prayer was not a way of blessing the bread so that it might become a vehicle of blessing to other people but rather an act of blessing, *i.e.* of thanking, God for his goodness in providing it. There was probably no special significance in the breaking and distribution of the bread; it was simply the ordinary way of dividing up a loaf so that each person present might have a share. Similarly, at the end of the meal the host took a cup of wine, known as 'the cup of blessing', and gave thanks to God for it, after which all present drank.

This description is of a formal meal at which guests were present. At an ordinary meal the use of wine was not obligatory, but the saying of the thanksgiving was essential.[9] Even if the description of the formal meal, which is based on rabbinic sources later than the New Testament, has been somewhat elaborated, the general principle that meals were accompanied by thanksgiving to God for what was eaten and drunk is certainly as old as the time of Jesus and the early church.

It will be noted that the 'elements' of bread and wine which characterise the Last Supper were present in a Jewish formal meal, and later we shall have to ask whether this kind of meal provides an adequate setting for the Christian meal. Meanwhile, however, we must mention in passing two particular types of meal which have been regarded by some scholars as providing a better background to the Last Supper.

First, H. Lietzmann, the author of a massive work on the history of the Lord's Supper, popularised the idea that there was a special kind of meal which could be held by a group of friends and had a religious character. There existed a number of groups, known as *haburoth*, whose members sought together to achieve ritual holiness and to undertake works of charity, and these groups met together for common meals.[10] The suggestion is then made that this kind of meal provided the model for the Last Supper. However, it has been emphasised by various scholars that there is no evidence whatever that the Jewish *haburoth* held meals that were in any way different from ordinary Jewish meals, and so this explanation of the origin of the characteristic features of the Last Supper should be dismissed from discussion.[11]

The same verdict must also be passed on the second suggestion, which is that the Last Supper was modelled on the Jewish custom of a special ritual to sanctify the Sabbath. What happened was that the head of the household would say over the cup of wine 'Blessed be he who has sanctified the Sabbath day'. This saying was uttered at the evening meal which immediately preceded sunset and the arrival of the Sabbath or a feast day, if the meal lasted through into the Sabbath, or it was said at a special ceremony if the meal had already finished. This blessing or *kiddush* was thus simply a blessing which accompanied the drinking of a cup of wine by the members of the household or was part of a meal. But the theory that Jesus' Supper was a *kiddush* meal[12] is impossible because there was no such thing as a *kiddush* meal other than the regular Jewish meal just before the Sabbath or a feast day, and also because the Sabbath *kiddush* took place on Friday evening by our reckoning, whereas Jesus held his Supper on Thursday evening. The theory of a special Passover *kiddush* on the evening before the usual festival supper is also an illusion.[13]

THE JEWISH PASSOVER MEAL

Since the Synoptic Gospels indicate that Jesus' Last Supper was in fact a Passover meal, we must look somewhat more closely at the features of this meal; even if some scholars are right in questioning whether the Supper was a Passover meal held at the proper time, we must still try to understand the background against which the Evangelists themselves present the Supper. The historical evolution of the Passover from its beginnings in Old Testament times to the form used in the time of Jesus is complicated,[14] and we do not need to trace it here; it will be sufficient for our purpose to outline how the festival was celebrated in New Testament times.[15]

There were in fact two festivals which were closely joined together. The feast of Unleavened Bread, which lasted for seven days, overlapped the feast of the Passover. The two feasts were held in the Jewish month of Nisan, which fell in March or April by our reckoning. On the thirteenth day of the month every scrap of leaven had to be removed from each house, and no leaven was allowed during the festival period which lasted until the twenty-first day of the month. The Passover itself was celebrated on the fifteenth day of the month, and the essential element in the celebration was the Passover meal. Since the Jewish day began at sunset, the meal was held in the evening at the beginning of the festival day. During the afternoon of what would be the same day by our reckoning but was the end of the fourteenth day by the Jewish reckoning the lambs which were intended for consumption at the Passover meal were brought to the temple and there they were personally slain by the persons offering them instead of, as was usual, by the priests. The priests took the blood from the slaughtered animals and poured it out at the foot of the altar, and they also burned the fat from them on the altar of burnt offering. Then the people gathered together in family groups or in *ad hoc* gatherings of friends, at least ten in number, to celebrate the meal after sunset.

The meal began as the head of the household spoke the words of thanksgiving for the feast day (*i.e.* the Passover *kiddush*) and for the wine over the first of a series of four cups of wine, and the wine was served to the guests.[16] This was followed by a preliminary course of *hors d'oeuvres*, greens, bitter herbs and *haroseth* sauce (a mixture of fruits and sauces in vinegar). The main course was served to the guests at this point, but according to J. Jeremias the guests did not start to eat it until the passover

haggadah had been said and the first part of the *hallel* was sung.[17]
The *hallel* was the cycle of Psalms which were sung at Passover,
and the first part consisted of Psalm 113 or Psalms 113–114.
The *haggadah*, a word which means 'narrative' in Hebrew, was
the Passover story, and it was a recital of the great events of
redemption as these were suggested by the symbolism employed
at the meal. It will be best simply to reproduce the actual wording from the Mishnah in order that we may gain some idea of the
spirit of the occasion as it was felt by the Jews:

> The son asks his father (and if the son has not enough
> understanding his father instructs him [how to ask]), 'Why is
> this night different from other nights? For on other nights we
> eat seasoned food once, but this night twice; on other nights
> we eat leavened or unleavened bread, but this night all is
> unleavened; on other nights we eat flesh roast, stewed,
> or cooked, but this night all is roast.' And according to
> the understanding of the son his father instructs him. He
> begins with the disgrace and ends with the glory; and he
> expounds from *A wandering Aramaean was my father* ...
> [Dt. 26:5–11] until he finishes the whole section.
>
> Rabban Gamaliel used to say: Whosoever has not said [the
> verses concerning] these three things at Passover has not ful-
> filled his obligation. And these are they: Passover, unleavened
> bread, and bitter herbs: 'Passover' – because God passed over
> the houses of our fathers in Egypt; 'unleavened bread' –
> because our fathers were redeemed from Egypt; 'bitter herbs'
> – because the Egyptians embittered the lives of our fathers in
> Egypt. In every generation a man must so regard himself as if
> he came forth himself out of Egypt, for it is written, *And
> thou shalt tell thy son in that day saying, It is because of that
> which the Lord did for me when I came forth out of Egypt.*
> Therefore are we bound to give thanks, to praise, to glorify,
> to honour, to exalt, to extol, and to bless him who wrought
> all these wonders for our fathers and for us. He brought us
> out from bondage to freedom, from sorrow to gladness, and
> from mourning to a Festival-day, and from darkness to great
> light, and from servitude to redemption; so let us say before
> him the *Hallelujah*.[18]

The second or main course of the meal began with the drinking of a second cup of wine, and with the saying of a grace,
spoken by the head of the household, over the unleavened bread
which was now served for the first time in the meal. The main

course consisted of the roasted Passover lamb, served with bitter herbs and fruit purée.

The meal was followed by a third cup of wine, known as the cup of blessing, and this was again accompanied by a grace. In a normal meal a dessert course would have been served at this point. This was apparently omitted in the Passover meal; in place of it the guests sang the second part of the *hallel*, Psalms 115 (or 114) to 118.

Finally, the fourth cup of wine was served, although some doubt has been expressed whether this custom goes back to the time of Jesus. After the meal was over, the guests were supposed to spend the night soberly in prayer.

The popularity of the Passover can be seen in the fact that an estimated 100,000 people were crowded into Jerusalem for it each year at the time of Jesus. The feast was primarily one of remembrance and praise to God for his redemption of the people of Israel from Egypt. It also became an occasion for looking forward to the future redemption which God would bring through the Messiah.

THE MEALS OF THE QUMRAN SECT

Although the Passover provides the most obvious background for the Last Supper of Jesus and his disciples, there are one or two other occasions in Judaism and the pagan world which must be taken into account as we try to see the meals of Jesus and his followers in their contemporary environment. Since the discovery of the Dead Sea Scrolls just over thirty years ago appeal has continually been made to them for any light that they may shed on the beliefs and practices of Jesus and the first Christians. The scrolls are the literary remains of a Jewish group which lived at Qumran at the north-west corner of the Dead Sea. They followed what we would regard as a monastic type of existence. They had gone out into the wilderness as a result of their disillusionment with the Judaism of their time, and sought to serve God by studying and keeping his law and living holy lives in separation from their fellow-Jews. Their number included priests, but we do not know whether they offered any sacrifices. They also followed a solar calendar which was at variance with the official Jewish lunar calendar, and as a result the proper dates for celebrating the Jewish feasts according to their calendar were out of step with the official dates.

What is of interest to us is the fact that they held communal

meals. The instructions which have survived relate to groups of
the sect wherever they may happen to meet, and, if the usual
identification of the sect as a type of Essenes is correct, this means
that Qumran was not the only place where the members might
gather and share meals together. The description of their meals
given to us by Josephus is not especially remarkable. Here is his
account of the Essene breakfast. It took place at the fifth hour of
the day after a period of work and a purifying bath in cold water:

> Pure now themselves, they repair to the refectory, as to
> some sacred shrine. When they have taken their seats in
> silence, the baker serves out the loaves to them in order, and
> the cook sets before each one plate with a single course.
> Before meat the priest says a grace, and none may partake
> until after the prayer. When breakfast is ended, he pronounces
> a further grace; thus at the beginning and at the close they
> do homage to God as the bountiful giver of life. Then laying
> aside their raiment, as holy vestments, they again betake them-
> selves to their labours until the evening. On their return they
> sup in like manner, and any guests who may have arrived
> sit down with them.[19]

With this account we may compare that which is given in one
of the Dead Sea Scrolls:

> In every place where there are ten persons of the Council
> of the Community, let there not lack among them a man who
> is a priest. And let them sit before him, each according to his
> rank, and in the same order let them ask their advice in every-
> thing. And then when they set the table to eat, or (prepare)
> the wine to drink, the priest shall first stretch out his hand to
> pronounce a blessing on the first-fruits of bread and wine.[20]

The description given in the Scroll is obviously not very different from that in Josephus's account of the Essenes, and it may
well be that the two writers are describing different forms of what
was essentially the same practice. In both cases the meal begins
with a grace, but in the Scrolls the grace is linked particularly
to bread and wine. The grace is said by a priest because the
Qumran community was a priestly community and therefore it
was a priest rather than a layman who was to take the part of the
head of the household. Apart from this feature, however, there is
at first sight nothing to distinguish the Qumran meal from the
ordinary Jewish meal described earlier. In the Qumran meal the

thanks for the bread and the thanks for the wine are linked together as if they were spoken at the beginning of the meal, but the text could be understood to refer to separate acts, as in the ordinary Jewish meal.

There may, however, be something more to the Qumran meal than this. First, a parallel has been drawn with the sacred meal of a Jewish sect called the Therapeutae who lived in Egypt; the meal of this group was regarded as having similarities to the eating of the shewbread by the priests in the temple. Hence it has been argued that the Qumran meal was derived from the practice of the priests in the temple.[21] There is, however, one important difference which rather weakens this theory. The Qumran meal included wine, whereas the meals of the priests who were on duty in the temple did not include wine.[22] Moreover, although the description of the meal in the Scroll refers only to bread and wine, there is no good reason to assume that these were the only things served; the bread and wine are particularly mentioned because these were the objects for which thanks were given to God as part of the usual Jewish ritual.

Second, we must also notice the existence of another passage in the Scrolls:

[Concerning the mee]ting of the men of renown [called] to assembly for the Council of the Community when [Adonai] will have begotten the Messiah among them.

[The Priest] shall enter [at] the head of all the Congregation of Israel, then all [the chiefs of the sons] of Aaron the priests called to the assembly, men of renown; and they shall sit [before him], each according to his rank.

And afterward, [the Mess]iah of Israel [shall enter]; and the chiefs of [the tribes of Israel] shall sit before him, each according to his rank, according to their [position] in their camps and during their marches; then all the heads of fa[mily of the Congre]gation, together with the wise me[n of the holy Congregation], shall sit before them, each according to his rank.

And [when] they gather for the Community tab[le], [or to drink w]ine, and arrange the Community table [and mix] the wine to drink, let no man [stretch out] his hand over the first-fruits of bread and [wine] before the Priest; for [it is he who] shall bless the first-fruits of bread and w[ine, and shall] first [stretch out] his hand over the bread. And after[wards], the Messiah of Israel shall [st]retch out his hands over the bread.

[And afterwards], all the Congregation of the Community shall [bl]ess, ea[ch according to] his rank.

And they shall proceed according to this rite at every mea[l where] at least ten persons [are as]sembled.[23]

This passage comes from a separate document and appears to envisage a time when the Messiah will have appeared and taken his place among the community. Even at this point the priest at the head of the community still retained his precedence over the Messiah who was a layman. The procedure at the meal is the same as in the previous description,[24] except for the note that the Messiah is next in precedence to the priest. M. Black has pointed out that the expectation of the Messiah coming may be based on the prophecy in Ezekiel 44 where the Prince enters the temple and sits there to eat bread before the Lord. He then suggests that the Qumran sectaries may have regarded their ordinary meals as anticipations of this future meal when the Messiah would be present with them. He also draws attention to a fragmentary text which refers to the eating of bread in the temple, and suggests that the sect looked forward to the restoration of the temple and its rites in the future.[25] This may well be so, but it must remain doubtful whether the ordinary meals of the sect were seen in this eschatological light; the point of the text about the future meal seems to be to say that, even when the Messiah comes, the priest still has precedence over him, rather than to suggest that the coming of the Messiah is an event of such magnitude that hope for it coloured every meal which was held. However, the fact that such meals were held by a group which looked forward to the future coming of the Messiah may perhaps constitute a parallel to the Christian church which looked forward to the return of the Messiah and celebrated the Lord's Supper 'until he comes'.[26]

THE STORY OF JOSEPH AND ASENATH

One further possible piece of Jewish background should probably be mentioned, since some writers have seen a clue to the origins of the Lord's Supper, or at least a possible influence on Christian practice, in it. This is the story of Joseph and Asenath, which has been handed down in a Greek version and is usually thought to be of Jewish origin.[27] The story is a romance which tells how Joseph met and eventually married Asenath, the daughter of an Egyptian priest. The main theme is the con-

version of Asenath to the Jewish faith. At first Joseph refused
to have anything to do with her, since he was, as the story says,
'a man who worships God, blesses with his mouth the living
God, eats the blessed bread of life, drinks the blessed cup of
immortality, and is anointed with the blessed oil of incorruption'.[28] When, however, Asenath repented, she was visited by an
angel: 'He stretched out his right hand and took a small piece
from the (honey)comb and ate, and with his own hand placed
what was left in Asenath's mouth and said to her, "Eat," and she
ate. And the angel said to her, "Lo! now you have eaten the
bread of life and drunk the cup of immortality and been anointed
with the oil of incorruption." '[29]

If this story is of Jewish origin and reflects Jewish practice,
then one might conclude from it that in some circles special
importance was attached to bread and wine together with oil.
It has been conjectured that the story may even indicate the
existence of an otherwise unknown Jewish initiation meal for
proselytes, and that it may testify to a form of Christian initiation, based on a Jewish pattern, which included anointing,
baptism and the Lord's Supper.[30] The story has been assigned to
the Therapeutae or Essenes, and thus brought into the thought-
world of the Dead Sea Scrolls.[31] However, it must be insisted
that the date and origin of the story of Joseph and Asenath
remain extremely uncertain; we know so little about this document that to use it to explain the Lord's Supper is a case of
obscurum per obscurius.[32]

PAGAN CULTIC MEALS

So far our discussion of background has been confined to the
Jewish world and we have said nothing about the possible
influence of pagan meals on the Lord's Supper. It would, however, be wrong to leave these out of account. It is true that pagan
meals are unlikely to have influenced the practice of Jesus
himself; although we must never forget that the Jews were a
minority group in their own land and were surrounded by pagans
who followed their own religions, there is nothing that would
suggest that Jesus himself was influenced by anything other than
Judaism. But the situation could well have been different once
the church moved out into the pagan world and its members
began to include former pagans. If such people had formerly
taken part in pagan rites, they could certainly have been tempted
to interpret what went on in the church meeting by analogy

with what went on in a pagan group, and the evidence of 1 Corinthians suggests that this is exactly what did happen.

Ancient religions, especially the Greek mystery religions, held cultic meals, as is apparent from Paul's answer in 1 Corinthians 8:10 to the question whether a Christian might sit at table in an idol's temple. A. D. Nock has listed three main types of such meal.[33]

First, there was the meeting of a group of adherents of a particular cult simply for fellowship together. Such meals might commemorate the dead founder of a particular group. H. Lietzmann suggested that the Christian concept of celebrating the Lord's Supper in memory of Jesus was derived from this pagan practice.[34] His suggestion has been criticised by J. Jeremias who has shown that the phraseology used in the pagan meals is different, that the pagan meals were held not on the anniversary of the death of the person honoured but generally on the birthday, and that such meals were becoming increasingly secular rather than religious in the first century. He concludes that it is unlikely that the pagan meals provide the origin of the motif of remembering Jesus.[35]

Second, there were meals at which a god or goddess was thought to preside. A second-century papyrus contains an invitation to a meal in the form: 'Chairemon invites you to eat at the table of the Lord Sarapis.' The language here is similar to that of Paul when he speaks of being partakers of the table of the Lord or of the table of demons (1 Cor. 10:21). Although S. Neill has warned against the easy assumption that the Christian language is based on the pagan language attested in a later text from Alexandria,[36] it remains probable that the normal Greek usage, which spoke of the 'table of God', has influenced the form of Paul's wording, especially since this phrase had already been used in the Septuagint for the Jewish altar (Ezk. 44:16; Mal. 1:7, 12).[37] What we are dealing with here is in fact a type of pagan meal which is also attested in the Old Testament, the holding of a meal after a sacrifice in which the worshippers eat the animal previously offered on the altar and thus have fellowship with the god. Paul's citation of Exodus 32:6 in 1 Corinthians 10:7 shows that he recognised the parallel between the idolatrous worship of the golden calf and pagan cults. The difference between the pagan and the Jewish meals was that in the former the worshippers were thought of as sharing the meal with the god but in the latter the worshippers ate in the presence of God.[38]

The third type of meal mentioned by Nock is the eating of the raw flesh of bulls in the cult of Dionysus; here the bull appears to have been regarded as a representation of the god, so that the worshippers were eating the god himself. But this rite of eating raw flesh is prehistoric, and we have no evidence that the meal had the same significance in the cult in historic times.

It is possible that eating and drinking in some other cults had a similar significance, but we know so little about these cults that it is impossible to draw any firm conclusions regarding the presence of this motif. There is no firm evidence for theophagy in the mysteries of Attis and Cybele, the cult of the Cabiri, or in Mithraism.[39] In any case, there is nothing in 1 Corinthians which suggests that thoughts of this kind played any part in the Lord's Supper. When Jesus speaks of eating his flesh and drinking his blood in John 6:53–56, the thought is clearly metaphorical and spiritual.

It emerges that the pagan background has nothing to do with the origins of the Lord's Supper. The one point where a parallel can be seen is in the pagan meals after sacrifices to which Paul explicitly refers in 1 Corinthians 10, but these meals were the ones which had parallels in Judaism, including above all the Passover meal itself. But we cannot use the mystery religions to throw light on the Lord's Supper since we have no reliable information about any aspects of them which would provide parallels to the Christian meal.

CHAPTER TWO

The Accounts of the Last Supper

Now that we have examined the background to the meals which were held by Jesus and by the early church, there are two possible routes that we can follow in our investigation. One is to begin by examining the evidence for what happened at the Lord's Supper held in the early church, and then to work backwards from that meal to the question of what gave rise to it, namely whether the early church was following a pattern set by Jesus at a meal with his disciples before he died. The alternative route is to begin with the Last Supper and then to trace the development forwards from it to the practice of the early church. If we had any serious historical doubts about the historicity of the Last Supper, its character and its exemplary significance for the early church, then clearly it would be necessary to begin with the known historical fact of the church's practice of holding the Lord's Supper and to work backwards from that point to what may have lain behind it. Right up to this day there are some scholars who take that attitude. The radical German scholar H. Braun can say: 'The final meal (Mk. 14:22-24) may be a reading back of the Lord's Supper as celebrated in Hellenistic Christian communities into the last days of Jesus, since the meal shows the marks of Hellenistic sacramental religion, and it is difficult to find a place for it in Palestinian or even in Qumran religious thinking.'[1] This view is not an original one. We find essentially the same position in the writings of R. Bultmann. He thinks that the sacramental meals held in the Hellenistic church were a transformation of the fellowship meals held in the Palestinian church which originated in the table-fellowship between Jesus and his disciples. But he argues that at first there was no special reference to a Last Supper held by Jesus; this arose only when the church moved out into the Hellenistic or Gentile world and it made use of what Bultmann calls 'an etiological cult-narrative' – a phrase which undoubtedly means that he regards the account of the Last Supper as being unhistorical.' Various other scholars adopt similar verdicts on the story of the Last Supper.[2]

Although the authority of R. Bultmann is very considerable in New Testament study, there is no need for us to be intimidated by him; one can cite scholars of equal standing who would strongly affirm the historicity of the Last Supper, even though they admit to varying degrees of certainty or uncertainty about the details of what took place. Foremost among these is J. Jeremias who has devoted a solid book of over 250 pp. to the question,[3] and his patient and detailed discussion of the matter cannot be overthrown simply by the brief, dogmatic statements of Bultmann. To be sure one cannot settle the question by merely citing authorities and counting heads. Nevertheless, there is sufficient evidence that there was a historical Last Supper to justify us in beginning there and attempting to build on it as a foundation for understanding the practice of the church. In the course of our discussion the reasons for adopting this position will become evident.

Nevertheless, there is some difference of opinion over what actually happened at the Last Supper, and we cannot escape the historical question of what kind of event lies behind our sources. We must, therefore, in a sense start with the early church and with the documents which it has bequeathed to us in order to discover what may be known about the Last Supper.

THE PROBLEM OF THE SOURCES

(1). *The Pauline account*

Our earliest datable source which describes the Last Supper is to be found in Paul's first letter to the church at Corinth. It is also our earliest evidence for the celebration of the Lord's

Supper in the church. When Paul had to discuss how this meal ought to be held and to correct certain abuses which had been reported to him, he based his comments on an account which he says that he 'received' from the Lord and 'delivered' to the Corinthian Christians. These words show that Paul was citing an existing form of words, and that he regarded it as a kind of official statement; he is using the same vocabulary as Jewish teachers used when they were passing on authoritative statements from past teachers which had first been passed on to them.[4] The fact that Paul was quoting a tradition in this passage, 1 Corinthians 11:23–5, is further evident from an examination of the wording; analysis has shown that the vocabulary and style is not that of Paul himself,[5] and, since there is not the slightest reason to suppose that the words were added by somebody else after Paul had finished the letter, and indeed everything points in the opposite direction, we can be quite certain that Paul is quoting a statement which he had received from other Christians. We may note further that Paul says that he had already told the Corinthians what he was now incorporating in his letter; that is to say, Paul must have passed on this tradition during the time which he spent in Corinth establishing the church, a period which can be accurately dated to within a year or so of AD 51.[6] This means that Paul's statement was in existence within some twenty years of the death of Jesus.

But where and when did Paul first hear this statement? When he says that he received it 'from the Lord', we are not to take this to mean a special divine revelation given to him. Rather he is referring to a tradition that was current in the church and which ultimately came from the Lord himself.[7] Obviously Paul heard it before he came to Corinth, and he must originally have heard it in some existing Christian church. There are only three real possibilities, Antioch, Damascus and Jerusalem. Antioch was the church from which Paul set out on his missionary work, and Damascus was the church with which he had his first Christian contacts after his conversion. Now these two churches were both founded by Christians from Jerusalem who took their knowledge of Christianity from Jerusalem, and we also know that Paul visited Jerusalem within three years of his conversion (Gal. 1:18). It is therefore extremely likely that Paul's knowledge of how the Lord's Supper should be celebrated goes back to the practice of the church in Jerusalem. This means that the onus of proof is on those who would deny that the formula cited by Paul goes back to the church in Jerusalem. In order to do so they would need to show that the formula has a Greek origin and that it reflects Greek ideas. But it has been shown that the formula contains signs of having been translated out of a Semitic language,[8] and we have already seen that there is no reliable evidence for the Hellenistic meals which Bultmann and others regarded as the pattern for the Lord's Supper.[9] It would seem to be time that this baseless speculation was dropped from the discussion. The probabilities are that Paul's formula goes back to Greek-speaking Christians in Jerusalem, who had translated it out of the story of the Last Supper used by Hebrew- or Aramaic-speaking Christians.[10] We are, then, on strong ground in tracing Paul's formula about the Last Supper right back to the very early days of the church, and this naturally increases our confidence in the historical value of this report.

(2). *Paul and the Synoptic narratives*

The tradition which is preserved by Paul is paralleled in the central sections of the description of Jesus' last meal in the synoptic Gospels, although they differ from one another in wording. However, the three synoptic accounts can be reduced to two for the purpose of comparison with Paul's tradition. This is because the differences between the accounts in Mark 14:22–25 and Matthew 26:26–28 are small and of such a kind that it is generally agreed that Matthew's account is a light revision of Mark's.[11] We are left, then, with the accounts in Mark and Luke.

The next stage is to observe that the account given by Paul is confined to the central elements in the Last Supper, the distribution of the bread and the cup and the sayings of Jesus which explain their significance. In the Gospels, however, these elements are found in the context of a fuller description of the preparations for the Passover meal, a saying or sayings of Jesus about the fact that he will not eat or drink again until the kingdom of God comes, and various other sayings which are reported in considerable detail in Luke. That is to say, what is given by Paul is an account of the particular part of the Last Supper which provided a pattern for the Lord's Supper, while the Gospels give us a historical report of the Last Supper in its context in the story of Jesus. This observation is confirmed by an examination of the precise contents of Paul's account in comparison with the parallel sections in the Gospels. Paul's account tells us what the Lord Jesus did on the night when he was betrayed as a pattern for the disciples to follow in remembrance of him. The Gospels by contrast are simply giving a historical account of the Last Supper, although their accounts also are admittedly selective and framed with an eye to their usefulness in the church. Thus Paul's account is about what Jesus did and the commands which he gave to the disciples, while the Gospels tell about what Jesus and the disciples did; again, the Gospels include Jesus' words about not eating or drinking again, but Paul leaves out this element which was not relevant to the celebration of the Lord's Supper.[12]

These points show that there is a difference in purpose between the Gospels and Paul. What Paul is giving us is 'the words of institution' which tell the church what to do when it celebrates the Supper. These instructions were handed down in a stereotyped form to provide the churches with the pattern which they were to follow. But in the Gospels we have a historical account of what happened at the Last Supper which forms part of an ongoing story of the last days of Jesus.

(3). *Liturgical or historical origin?*

If so, which came first, the liturgical account or the historical account? Obviously if the event is historical, then *a* historical report (which need not necessarily have been in the wording found in any of our present accounts) provided by somebody who was at the Last Supper must have come first. But is our oldest source liturgical? In favour of this view it has been urged that the passages in the Gospels which are parallel to Paul's account can be regarded as detachable from their contexts. In Mark 14:22 the central account begins with the words 'as they were eating', which repeat a similar form of words found four verses earlier in 14:18. This awkward repetition has suggested that Mk. 14:22–25 is an insertion into the account of Jesus' meal with his disciples, a meal which lacked the 'sacramental' features found in this 'insertion'.[13] The same kind of argument has been applied to Luke's narrative. Here we have an account of a Pass-over meal at which Jesus shared a cup of wine with the disciples *before* the distribution of the bread and cup with the words of interpretation (Lk. 22:15–18/19–20).[14] It has been argued that these are two separate accounts of the same meal, and even that the two accounts of Jesus' giving a cup of wine to the disciples are descriptions of the giving of one and the same cup.[15] Hence we have the hypothesis that the part of the story in the Gospels which records the words of institution is in fact taken from a liturgical account, similar to that found in Paul, and has been inserted in the appropriate context in the Gospels.[16] On this view, the oldest form of the central account is a liturgical formula. In my commentary on Luke I stated that this was a feasible hypothesis, but I pointed out that there was good reason to suppose that the liturgical account was based on a fuller account which contained some allusion to the Passover, reflected in Paul's knowledge that the cup of wine at the Last Supper was the 'cup of blessing' (1 Cor. 10:16) and in the trace of the forward look to the future kingdom of God in Paul's phrase 'until he comes'. On this view, what happened was that a putative longer account of the central actions at the Last Supper had been replaced in the Gospels by the present insertion which had been somewhat adapted as a result of its use as a liturgical formula.[17]

Further consideration of the matter leads to a different conclusion. First, we have already noticed that the accounts in the Gospels are less well adapted for liturgical use than Paul's account. It is probable that the liturgical formula in Paul is derived from an account of the type found in the Gospels. Second, it has been argued that the Marcan account is not an awkward insertion; the words 'as they were eating' are a historical comment at the appropriate point in the story to indicate that what Jesus did took place during the Passover meal when the bread was served.[18] Third, it has also been argued that the Lucan account is a unified story of the various stages in the meal and does not consist of two separate traditions.[19] Without going into detail, it can be said that all of these arguments are cogent. They show that the form of the accounts in the Gospels is not basically liturgical and that the accounts are not insertions which have replaced earlier accounts; the Gospel accounts are the historical narratives (or at least the kind of historical narratives) from which developed the liturgical formula found in Paul. This is an important conclusion because it shows that the origin of the words of institution was not in a liturgical formula but in a historical account. In other words, the theory that the story of the Last Supper arose as a cult-aetiology, a story that was invented to explain why the church carried out a ritual that had a different origin, is impossible on form-critical grounds.

THE RELATION BETWEEN THE SOURCES

We have now reached the conclusion that a historical account of the Last Supper, as found in the Gospels, lies behind the more liturgical account of the institution of the Lord's Supper, as found in 1 Corinthians. This of course does not necessarily mean that the account in any one of the Gospels is an earlier formulation than Paul's account, especially since 1 Corinthians is an older document than any of the Gospels and since the formula itself is much older than the Epistle in which it is found. We are still left, therefore, with the problem of trying to work back to the earliest form of the narrative.

(1). *Possible solutions*

It is safe to say that every possible solution to the problem has found supporters. (a). The view that Paul's account is more primitive than that in the Gospels has commanded much support and could perhaps be said to have been dominant in research until recently.[20] (b). The claims of Mark to preserve the original account have been defended by J. Jeremias, and this view has attracted many followers.[21] (c). A new feature was introduced into the discussion by H. Schürmann who argued in great detail that Luke's account was not, as was often thought, an amalgam of the Marcan and Pauline accounts, but rather an independent account which had strong claims to be the oldest form of the narrative.[22] (d). Over against these claims that any one source represents the oldest form of the tradition we have the view that the different sources bear testimony to a primitive form from which they have all developed in varied ways; the earliest form is, therefore, a matter for reconstruction, and it is debated whether we can carry out the task of reconstructing it with any certainty.[23] To the casual observer the differences between the three accounts in question may seem comparatively trivial, so that a choice between these various possibilities is not a matter of great consequence; nevertheless, we must make some investigation of the problem as a basis for a closer study of what actually happened at the Last Supper.

(2). *The longer and shorter texts of Luke*

The comparison of the accounts is complicated by the fact that one of them has been handed down to us in various different forms in the manuscripts. The passage in question is Luke 22:19-20. The great majority of the MSS give us a text which contains a full account of the words of Jesus over the bread and his words over the cup of wine, and which is thus parallel to the texts in Mark and 1 Corinthians. But a small group of textual authorities omit verses 19b–20, leaving an account in which after the first cup of wine and Jesus' saying that he will not drink again of the fruit of the wine we have the distribution of the bread and a brief comment by Jesus over it, and then nothing more. The rest of the saying over the bread ('which is given for you'), the distribution of the wine and the accompanying saying are all omitted, and the narrative goes straight on to the prophecy of Jesus' betrayal.

This shorter form of the text is undoubtedly the 'harder' or more difficult reading, and it has consequently attracted much scholarly support. In fine, it is easier to suppose that an original 'short' version of the narrative was expanded by scribes on the basis of the parallel accounts than that an original 'complete' version of the story was drastically curtailed at its central point. This basic argument can be strengthened by the observation that the short text is attested at an early date in various other textual authorities which rearrange the order of the material in order to put the distribution of the bread and the wine into the correct sequence. Further, it is not impossible to advance reasons for supposing that the short text represents what Luke is likely to have written. Since, it is argued, he had an aversion to an 'atonement' theology (as, it is suggested, may be seen by comparing his version of the saying of Jesus in Mk. 10: 45 in Lk. 22: 27 and by noting the omission of any theology of atonement in Acts, except for the vestige in Acts 20: 28), he could have deliberately omitted a reference here to Jesus' death for others. Alternatively, he may have wished to alter the account of the institution of the Lord's Supper into an account of the last Passover meal held by Jesus and to underline its paschal character.[24]

However, the case for retaining the longer form of the text is also strong. A point of particular importance is that the manuscript evidence for the short text is poor. It consists of only one Greek MS (D) and some Latin versions, together with some Syriac and Coptic evidence for rearranging the verses, and a variant reading with only one Greek MS (a decidedly erratic one!) in its favour is decidedly weak. How, we may ask, did all the other Greek MSS come to share the same longer text? Second, it has been argued that the additional wording in the longer form of the text is not based on Paul but represents a more primitive source.[25] The argument has been criticised,[26] but it seems probable that at least it still demonstrates that the Lucan text is unlikely to be due to a scribe who was assimilating the text to that of Paul. Third, the short text is extremely abrupt, and we are faced with the problem of explaining why Luke would have composed it. The argument that he wanted to avoid any reference to the atoning death of Jesus is quite unconvincing since Luke has left other references to the death of Jesus for the disciples untouched.[27] If Luke wished to underline the paschal character of the Last Supper, he could certainly have done this without surrendering the other aspects of the meal; that is to say, Luke's paschal stress does not explain why he would have omitted the verses in question.

The major difficulty if we regard the long text as original is to account for the development of the short text. J. Jeremias made a valiant attempt to argue that the church wished to preserve the secrecy of the words of institution and therefore abbreviated the text,[28] but this explanation seems very unlikely since nothing similar has taken place in the other three versions of the narrative. A second possibility is that the omission reflects liturgical practice in the second century.[29] Yet another possibility is that scribes were confused by the mention of two cups in Luke's account and dropped mention of the second one.[30] An important consideration is that the Greek MS which omits the verses in question also omits other phrases from the text of Luke, about whose authenticity there can be no question; that is to say, the omission may well be due to some idiosyncrasy of one particular scribe.[31] It is difficult to be certain which of these explanations is the correct one, and it may be that we should accept a combination of the fourth and the second or third. In any case, it seems to me that we do have sufficient reason to regard the longer text of Luke as being authentic, and to pursue our further investigation on this basis.[32]

(3). *Some general considerations*

Our next question, therefore, concerns the relationship of the Marcan, Lucan and Pauline accounts to one another. This is a particularly difficult problem to solve, and any proper discussion of it must inevitably be highly technical. We can do nothing more than indicate some of the general points that are relevant to a solution of the problem.

First, it must be emphasised that there is no good reason for supposing that any one of the three versions must necessarily be closer at all points to the original form of the account than the others. Each of the three versions can in theory preserve different features of the hypothetical original account, so that a reconstruction of this basic account could contain features drawn from all three surviving versions.

Second, from a literary point of view the Pauline account is the oldest form which we have, and therefore there is a certain presumption that it is closest to the original form. On the other hand, however, it is also the form which has been influenced by liturgical considerations more than the other, and hence it is quite possible that, although the accounts in the Gospels were committed to writing at a later date, they may be better witnesses to the original wording of the account.

Third, a factor which is often brought into the discussion is the number of Semitic features in each of the accounts. It can be assumed with certainty that the sayings of Jesus at the Last Supper were in either Aramaic or Hebrew,[33] and it is highly probable that the first account of the meal was given in one of these languages rather than in Greek. Consequently, our Greek versions of the account are translations, and one may look for features which suggest a literal translation from Aramaic or Hebrew into Greek. In the process of transmission such tell-tale signs of translation would be smoothed away and a better Greek style would result; hence the relative number of Semitisms in the different accounts may be a pointer to which is the earliest form of the tradition. The assessment of the narratives in this way by J. Jeremias has shown that Mark has the most Semitisms, Luke comes next, and Paul has least.[34] This argument would point to Mark's having preserved the most original form of the account. We shall, however, see that this argument must be treated with some caution.

Fourth a most important consideration concerns the nature of the Lucan account. The older view of the matter recognised that there are places where the wording of Luke is close to that of Mark and others where it is close to that of Paul, and consequently it was argued that Luke's text was based on the text of Mark which he had edited in the light of the variant form of the tradition preserved by Paul. If this is a correct reading of the evidence, then Luke's account can be dismissed from consideration, and we are left with Mark and Paul as our two remaining firsthand sources. This view has recently been strongly defended by R. Pesch.[35]

However, some twenty-five years earlier an impressive new hypothesis was developed by H. Schürmann. He argued in minute detail that in addition to the account in Mark Luke had access to another source which he made use of throughout his account of the Last Supper. In the central part of the narrative, which is our concern at the moment, Luke's source was close in wording to Paul but actually contained a more primitive form of the story, and Schürmann claimed that this form represented the nearest that we could attain to the original narrative; more recently Schürmann has retracted somewhat, and apparently no longer claims that Luke represents word for word the original account.[36] However, if Schürmann is right, this means that we cannot lay Luke aside but on the contrary must regard this account as an important early witness to the original form of the narrative.

The vital question is clearly whether Schürmann is correct in asserting that Luke's narrative is dependent upon an earlier form of the tradition used by Paul rather than upon the form attested by Paul. Pesch's discussion of this question is formulated as a criticism of Schürmann's argument, but in my opinion it is not successful. He fails to deal with two points. First, he does not manage to refute Schürmann's claim that there are a number of places where Luke's wording cannot be explained as a revision of Paul's wording, but represents a more primitive form of it.[37] Second, he does not answer Jeremias's argument that the style of Luke 22:19–20 is not Lucan but represents a source used by Luke.[38] If our assessment of the situation is correct, it follows that we cannot exclude the text of Luke from consideration and confine ourselves to a comparison of Mark and Paul, but rather that all three texts may contain original features of the narrative.

AN ANALYSIS OF THE TEXTS

With these considerations in mind, we can now attempt a preliminary inspection of the texts, confining ourselves for the moment to the central element in the narrative where all three sources run parallel. (See Table 2)

(1). *The distribution of the bread*

Mark's account commences with the words 'And as they were eating, he took bread, and blessed, and broke it, and gave it to them, and said.' This is the natural way of beginning the story in its context where the preparations for a meal have been described, and we have been told that Jesus and the Twelve had gathered together and had begun their meal. The repetition of the phrase 'as they were eating' from Mark 14:18 has been thought to be awkward, and a sign that the account has been interpolated into the description of the meal as a whole. It is, however, unlikely that a separate account of the words of institution began in this abrupt way, and it is more likely that the phrase is a transition within a connected narrative.[39] Paul's account begins with the words: 'The Lord Jesus on the night when he was betrayed took bread, and when he had given thanks, he broke it, and said'. This reads like the beginning of an independent account which could stand by itself as a liturgical rubic; if our argument is correct that the original account of the Last Supper was a historical report rather than a liturgical rubric, then it would follow that Paul's form here represents a revision of the original beginning of the story to make it capable of standing on its own.[40] Luke's account has a simple 'and' in place of the introductory phrases in Mark and Paul. Luke is thus closer to Mark than to Paul here, but whether his wording is more original than Mark's is hard to say; it may well be that to talk of relative originality here is to ask the wrong kind of question.[41]

The remainder of the introduction contains five elements which are common to all three accounts, except for the comment that Jesus gave the bread to the disciples, which is absent from Paul. Schürmann has attempted to show that Paul is describing a quasi-ritual action by Jesus which was important even if nobody received the elements, but he himself has to admit that the eating and drinking were important for Paul.[42] A better suggestion is that the concept of breaking the bread naturally included the thought of distributing it (Mk. 8:19).[43]

The only other difference between the accounts, apart from some syntactical points, is that Mark has the verb 'blessed', while Luke and Paul have 'gave thanks'. There is, however, no basic difference of meaning between these two verbs. 'To give thanks' and 'to bless' are alternative Greek translations for the Hebrew verb 'to bless, sc. God'; the latter is the literal translation, while the former brings out paraphrastically the fact that to bless God or to say the blessing meant to give thanks to God. The equivalence of the two words can be seen in their use side by side in Mark 14:22f. 'To give thanks' is more of a native Greek usage, and this verb became common in Christian usage for giving thanks at table. It must remain doubtful which of the two verbs stood in a hypothetical original Greek account of the meal,[44] if indeed there was but one standard Greek version.

(2). *The distribution of the cup*

Since the words of interpretation over the bread pose problems which cannot be solved without a consideration of the words over the cup, it will be simplest to look at the narrative framework of the second saying at this stage. Mark's account is closely parallel to the account of the distribution of the bread: 'And he took a cup, and when he had given thanks he gave it to them, and they all drank of it. And he said to them'. Luke and Paul have a much briefer introduction in more or less the same words: 'And the cup likewise after supper/Likewise also the cup after supper'. There is no verb in the Lucan/Pauline form, and we must supply some such words as 'he took, gave thanks for it, and gave it to them' from the earlier description of the distribution of the bread.

In favour of the originality of the Marcan form it can be argued that the longer wording was more likely to be abbreviated than vice versa, and that the Lucan/Pauline form has the effects of concentrating attention on the words of Jesus rather than the act of distribution and of putting more emphasis on the distribution of the bread, an emphasis which would be appreciated in communities where wine was not always available for the Lord's Supper.[45]

However, it can be argued in favour of the Lucan/Pauline form that Mark shows a tendency to assimilate the original, brief formula to the wording of the distribution of the bread. The earliness of the shorter formula can be seen in the echo of it in John 6:11. Of particular importance is the phrase 'after supper' which indicates correctly that the cup of wine in question came at the end of the meal, so that the distribution of the bread and the distribution of the wine were separated by the main part of the meal. This separation of the two actions soon ceased in the early church, if indeed it was ever the custom; they were placed together and seen in parallelism to each other.[46] This means that the preservation of the phrase 'after supper' at a time when the church's meal was celebrated in a different manner points to its early composition.[47] We have, then, evidence which points to the early existence of the Lucan/Pauline form.

A decision between the two forms of the wording is not easy. Logically, the fuller account, as preserved by Mark, is presupposed by Paul's account; in other words, it is difficult to imagine anybody telling the story for the first time in the Pauline manner, but it is easy to accept that at a subsequent stage abbreviation took place. On the other hand, it is very odd that in a liturgical rubric, which in effect tells people what to do, the precise way of dealing with the cup (which was not exactly 'likewise' with the way of dealing with the bread) is not given in detail. It is, therefore, on the whole more probable that the Marcan form is a later development from the Pauline, but one which brings us back to the earliest form.[48] This means that, so far as the action described is concerned, both accounts are in full agreement, except that Paul's account makes it clear that the distribution of the cup took place at the end of the meal.[49]

(3). *The sayings over the bread and the cup*

The problems of ascertaining the original wording of the sayings of Jesus, which are variously recorded in the sources, are extraordinarily difficult, and any solution must remain hypothetical. In essence the varying reports of the sayings contain the same basic elements. First of all, we must set out the differences which require explanation.

(a). The saying over the bread begins with a verb of command 'Take' in Mark; this is missing in Luke and Paul.

(b). All our texts contain the words 'This is my body', which are thus the most firmly attested part of the whole tradition.

(c). Luke and Paul have an explanatory phrase 'which is given (Paul omits 'given') for you'; this has no equivalent in Mark.

(d). At this point Luke and Paul both have the command 'Do this in remembrance of me'. This is repeated by Paul after the interpretation of the cup, but Mark does not have it at all. We shall consider this part of the saying separately later.

(e). The saying over the cup takes the form 'This is my blood of the covenant' in Mark; this wording appears to echo Exodus 24:8, 'Behold the blood of the covenant which the Lord has made with you.' In Luke and Paul, however, we have the form 'This cup is the new covenant in my blood'. Here 'This' is identified explicitly as the cup, and the cup (or its contents)[50] typifies not the blood which inaugurates the covenant but the covenant which is inaugurated by the blood; the addition of the word 'new' produces an allusion to Jeremiah 31:31.

(f). Mark adds the explanatory phrase 'which is poured out for many'; this echoes Isaiah 53:12. In Mark the phrase fits grammatically into the sentence as a description of the blood. Paul has nothing corresponding to the phrase, but Luke has the equivalent phrase 'which is poured out for you', which must refer logically to the blood of Jesus but which is loosely attached syntactically.[51] This phrase is parallel to the phrase 'which is

given for you' which is part of the saying over the bread in Luke
and Paul.

These are the differences between the sayings, and our
problem is to determine whether we can find an original form
that lies behind the different forms of the sayings and to explain
how the differences arose.

The initial command in Mark's form of the saying over the
bread can be discussed in isolation from the other differences.
If we take the absence of the word as the original form, the command in Mark can be regarded as a liturgical direction which
has crept into the saying. At a Jewish meal it was not normal to
tell the guests to take the bread in this rather formal manner.
The fact that liturgical directions of this kind developed in the
church can be seen from the fact that Matthew adds the further
command 'eat' to the saying. However, it can also be argued that
the verb belongs to the original historical setting of the Last
Supper, especially if Jesus was encouraging his disciples to eat
while he abstained from doing so.[52] This, however, must remain
uncertain. A stronger point is that earlier in Luke's account
(Lk. 22:17) the same command is found with the distribution
of the cup of wine. This suggests that the command did figure
in the sayings of Jesus, and in any case it is perfectly probable
that Jesus used it in the content of his new interpretation of the
bread and the cup.[53] The omission of the command in the
Lucan/Pauline version of the saying may be because it was felt
to be unnecessary, since it is implied in the act of distribution,
and perhaps because it seemed redundant alongside the command to 'do this' in remembrance of Jesus.[54] If Luke 22:15–17
is more primitive than Mark 14:25, it is possible that the command has 'floated' from one saying to the other.[55] On the whole,
it would be unwise to deny the possible originality of the command, but in any case the essential fact expressed by it is contained in the distribution of the bread by Jesus to the disciples.

The remaining differences between the sayings are intercon-
nected and must be discussed together. There are two main
problems: did the phrase 'which is given/poured out for many/
you' originally belong to the bread-saying or the cup-saying or
both or neither of them, and is the Marcan or the Lucan/
Pauline form of the first part of the cup-saying original?

If we assume that the Marcan form of the sayings is original,
we can account for the development of the Lucan/Pauline form
in this manner: First of all, there was a change in the cup-
saying from 'this is my blood of the covenant' to 'this cup is

the new covenant in my blood'. The claim that the development took place in this direction rather than the reverse is based on the following points. First, it has been argued that the Marcan form of the saying could have been understood by Jewish hearers as a reference to drinking blood, a thought which was so repulsive to them that an attempt could have been made to soften the wording.[56] Second, at the same time there could have been a desire to indicate clearly that the covenant of which Jesus spoke was the new covenant of Jeremiah 31:31.[57] Third, it has been argued that the reference to blood in the Lucan/Pauline form cannot have been derived from Jeremiah 31, but must have come from Exodus 24:8. That is to say, the Lucan/Pauline form presupposes the saying in its Marcan form with its explicit reference to Exodus 24:8 and is a theological elaboration of it.[58]

The second stage in the development was the formation of the phrase 'which is (given) for you' as a parallel to the phrase 'which is poured out for many'. In this way the brief bread-saying 'This is my body', which cried out for some elucidation, was filled out and made parallel to the cup-saying.[59] But at the same time this change in the bread-saying made the original phrase in the cup-saying redundant, and in any case the earlier change in the cup-saying now made the phrase syntactically awkward; consequently it was dropped. The fact that the phrase originally belonged to the cup-saying is demonstrated, first, by the difficulty of explaining how it ever came to be dropped from the bread-saying if it had originally been present there;[60] second, by the fact that the Marcan version has the more primitive form 'for many', which reflects Isaiah 53:12, while the Lucan/Pauline form has 'for you', which reflects liturgical usage in the early church;[61] and, third, in the fact that the linking of the phrase to 'this is my body' is said to produce a phrase that would be unintelligible in Aramaic.[62]

The third stage is seen in the replacement of the phrase 'which is poured out for you' at the end of the cup-saying in Luke's version. The secondary nature of the addition can be seen in the harsh syntactical connection, and the motive for it lay in the desire to produce parallelism with the new form of the bread-saying.[63] However, since we had to postulate something like the Lucan form as a halfway stage between the Marcan and Pauline forms, it is possible that the Lucan form is earlier than the Pauline form.

Although this account of the development sounds plausible, it is also possible to present a case for what is essentially the reverse process. If we begin with the Lucan/Pauline version, it can be argued that the lack of symmetry between the first parts of the bread-saying and the cup-saying led to a reformulation of the cup-saying to give it a form parallel to the bread-saying; as a result of this process the allusion to Exodus 24:8 became all the clearer and the word 'new' was dropped, since a reference to a covenant established by Jesus' blood would *ipso facto* be to a different covenant from the Mosaic one and could only be to the new covenant of Jeremiah.[64] The next part of the process was the dropping of the phrase 'which is given for you' from the bread-saying. This omission presupposes the inclusion of the phrase 'which is poured out for many' in the cup-saying. If we assume the originality of the Pauline form of the cup-saying, then we must assume that it was extended on the analogy of the bread-saying, and that then the bread-saying itself was shortened to the simple 'This is my body', with the result that all the weight of interpretation was placed on the cup-saying in the Marcan form.[65] On this view, the fuller form of the cup-saying in Luke is a combination of the Pauline and Marcan forms by an author who was determined not to lose any of the traditional wording. If, however, we assume the originality of the longer Lucan form of the cup-saying, then we can explain the Pauline form as an abbreviation of it to remove a phrase which was both stylistically awkward and also redundant alongside the fuller form of the bread-saying; we can also explain the Marcan form of the cup-saying as a simplification of the first part of the Lucan form which has the effect of removing the stylistic awkwardness.

We have thus three basic explanations of the development. Explanation A. (see Table 3) proceeds from the originality of the Marcan wording. Explanations B. and C. proceed from the originality of the Lucan/Pauline wording, the former assuming the originality of the form behind the Pauline account, and the latter assuming the originality of the form behind the Lucan account. How do we decide between these possibilities? Let us go over the supporting arguments.

First, we must deal with the question of Semitic background. It has already been observed that the greater number of Semitisms in the Marcan form may be a sign of its being closer to the original narrative.[66] This argument fails to recognise that the Marcan and Lucan/Pauline forms could both be translations out of Aramaic, the former by a more literal and the latter by a less literal translator. If both versions are dependent on a Greek tradition, then it must be admitted that Mark's form is more Semitic. In this case, however, the Lucan/Pauline form could have been Graecised in the course of transmission, while the Marcan tradition remained closer to its Aramaic original. Thus the question of the relative number of Semitisms is not of decisive importance for our investigation. A further point is that, despite contentions to the contrary, any of the forms of the sayings is possible in Aramaic, and we cannot settle the question of originality by claiming that certain forms are impossible in Aramaic.[67]

Second, it was argued that the Marcan form of the cup-saying could have been altered to avoid the impression that the Christians were drinking blood. In fairness it should be observed that the cup contained wine which represented blood rather than blood itself. It is important that in John 6:53–56 the actual thought of drinking blood is expressed in a bold metaphor. This can be taken in two ways. On the one hand, the passage shows that a Christian Evangelist had no compunction about recording the words of Jesus in this form. This could be used as an argument that the community would not have felt it necessary to alter a milder form of words. On the other hand, the Johannine passage reports that Jesus did speak in this way, and that it shocked the Jews. It can, therefore, be used as evidence that this form of Jesus' words is original. In short, we have here some evidence for the originality of the Marcan form of the cup-saying, but the case that it was altered to avoid the possibly repulsive implication of drinking blood is weaker. However, since the Lucan/Pauline cup stands for its contents, *i.e.* wine, and since the wine can hardly stand for a covenant but rather for the blood which inaugurates the covenant, it could be argued that this form of the saying is also open to the same misunderstanding as the Marcan saying. The argument for Marcan priority in these terms is a weak one. The important fact which has emerged, however, is that the Johannine tradition stands closer to the Marcan form.

Third, the reference to the 'new' covenant has been seen as the key to the change in the cup-saying. It is argued that the desire to produce a contrast to the Sinai covenant has led to making the covenant the logical subject of the saying and to the insertion of the word 'new'. However, if the main desire was to get a reference to Jeremiah 31:31 into the Marcan text, it is difficult to see why this could not have been done simply by inserting the adjective 'new' at the appropriate point.[68] The Pauline form does not seem to have any real advantages over the Marcan form, and I find it hard to envisage why the complicated change was thought necessary simply in order to get a clearer reference to the new covenant.

Fourth, we come to the claim that the phrase 'which is poured out for many' was transferred from the cup-saying to the bread-saying in an appropriate form. It was argued that it is difficult to see why it was ever dropped from the bread-saying if it originally belonged there. Two points arise here. First, the argument under consideration recognises that the bread-saying was felt to be inadequate without some interpretation of the word 'body'. If we now bear in mind that the bread-saying at the Last Supper was separated from the cup-saying by the length of the meal, the bread-saying in its short form must have been extremely cryptic, and we must ask whether Jesus is likely to have spoken so cryptically. Once, however, the two sayings were brought together in the church's liturgical action and rubric, the bread-saying could be understood in the light of the immediately following cup-saying, and hence the interpretative phrase was no longer necessary with the bread-saying. This, then, is an argument that the phrase originally belonged to the bread-saying.[69] This argument also effectively disposes of the objection that the dropping of the phrase from the bread-saying in the Marcan tradition is inconceivable if it was originally present there. Once the bread-saying and the cup-saying were brought together, the bread-saying could be understood in the light of the cup-saying.[70]

There is, however, an important point which could neutralise our claim. It can be argued that the action of Jesus in distributing the bread could be regarded as giving the interpretation of his body: just as the bread is distributed among the disciples, so his body could be understood as being in some sense for them; in this case, the action of distribution could have served the same purpose as the interpretative phrase and rendered the latter unnecessary.[71] But although this understanding of the action makes sense in the light of our knowledge of the saying, it seems unlikely that it would have made sense to the disciples apart from the saying. We conclude that there are strong grounds for arguing that the original bread-saying must have contained some element of interpretation, rather than that supplementation took place in the process of tradition.

Fifth, there is the point that the Marcan form 'for many' is older than the Lucan/Pauline 'for you'. It is true that the originality of 'for you' has been defended by Schürmann,[72] on the grounds that the church was unlikely to obscure an original allusion to Isaiah 53:12 and that the original saying would have made it clear that the blessings promised were for the actual people present. However, Jeremias's case for the originality of 'for many' on linguistic grounds seems the stronger.[73] But, even if the Marcan *wording* 'for many' is the older, this does not necessarily prove that Mark's *positioning* of the phrase is the older, and it is not impossible that the Lucan/Pauline positioning of the phrase is original.

Sixth, there is the question whether 'this is my body which is (given) for you' is a possible phrase in Aramaic. Here the argument of Schürmann seems cogent, when he claims that behind the wording lies the thought of the Servant who gives himself as a ransom for the many.[74]

This examination of the arguments for a development from the Marcan form to the Lucan/Pauline form has shown that they are far from convincing. We must now examine the arguments for development in the reverse direction.

First, it seems cogent to argue that the lack of symmetry between the bread-saying and the cup-saying could have led to assimilation between the two. The effect of the change was to move from the asymmetrical 'This is my body/This cup is the new covenant' to the symmetrical 'This is my body/This is my blood'. It would require a very strong argument to refute the claim that a postulated original symmetry of 'body/blood' is unlikely to have been changed to 'body/covenant'. This point has been challenged. It has been claimed that it is being assumed that 'body' and 'blood' are correlative terms like 'flesh' and 'blood', but in fact they are not so and really mean 'my body' and 'my dying'.[75] Hence there would have been no loss of symmetry in altering an original 'body/blood'. But the challenge cannot be sustained. For, first, if 'my blood' means 'my dying', it would also seem that 'my body' means 'my dying', especially in the light of the fuller phrase 'my body which is given for you'. Further, the 'body/blood' contrast reappears in John 6:53–56 as 'flesh/blood', and the possibility cannot be completely excluded that the original Aramaic word used by Jesus referred to his flesh.[76] Even if we reject this view, however, it seems clear that from the beginning the word 'body' was understood in terms of self-giving in death, so that there was a parallelism, rather than a correlation, between 'body' and 'blood'. In other words, the reference to a correlation between the terms may well be a red herring, and the point which remains unrefuted is that there was a parallelism between the two statements 'This is my

body' and 'This is my blood' which, once it had been established,
was unlikely to be disturbed. The original point thus still stands,
and it speaks powerfully against a development from the Marcan
form to the Lucan/Pauline form of words.

Second, there is the question whether the Lucan/Pauline
allusion to the *new* covenant of Jeremiah 31:31 would have been
dropped from the cup-saying if it had originally been part of it.
This is quite possible, since the Marcan form of the saying
still implies that Jesus is establishing a different covenant from
the Mosaic one.

Third, there is the problem of the dropping of the phrase
'which is given for you' from the bread-saying. The objection
is that this would destroy the parallelism which was being
created between the two sayings and thus go against the principle
that the trend in the tradition was towards the creation of symmetry rather than its removal. In this case, however, what was
being removed was not the parallelism of like clauses but rather
the redundancy caused by the presence of essentially identical
phrases.

Fourth, there is the problem of explaining the presence of the
phrase 'which is poured out for many' in the Marcan cup-saying.
If the Pauline form of the cup-saying, which does not contain
this phrase, is original, then we must assume that in the Marcan
tradition the cup-saying was first extended on the analogy of the
bread-saying in its Pauline form, and that then the bread-saying
was abbreviated; to put it otherwise, the phrase 'which is for
you' (in its hypothetical pre-Pauline form 'which is given for
many') was transferred from the bread-saying to the cup-saying
with appropriate changes in wording. The Lucan form of the
cup-saying is then a secondary combination of the Pauline and
Marcan forms. This transfer is certainly a possible one.

However, it may be easier to assume the originality of the
Lucan form of the cup-saying, in which case the Marcan tradition has simply taken over the original wording attested by Luke.
The argument against this assumption is that the Lucan phrase
is stylistically awkward in relation to the earlier part of the cup-
saying. This, however, may be a sign not of a clumsy conflation
of two traditions but rather of a primitive phrase which has been
tidied up in different ways in the Pauline and Marcan forms of
the tradition.[77]

We have now examined the arguments for the various patterns
of development. It appears that neither of the two main patterns,
from Mark to Luke/Paul and vice versa, can be defended by

invincible arguments. On balance I am inclined to favour the greater originality of the Lucan/Pauline wording. The wiser conclusion, however, is that the precise original form of the sayings and the history of their development cannot be reconstructed with certainty. What we can be confident about is the fact that the basic elements incorporated in the various forms of the sayings are primitive, even if we cannot be sure just how they were linked together.

In short, we may be confident that Jesus spoke of the bread as representing his body; that he likened the cup to his blood of the covenant or to the new covenant in his blood; and that he spoke of giving himself or pouring out his blood for the many.

(4). *The command to repeat the action*

We saw that the command 'Do this in remembrance of me' is found as part of the bread-saying in Luke and Paul and also as part of the cup-saying in Paul, but is missing from Mark. The repetition of the command in Paul is generally thought to be an addition due to a striving after parallelism between the two sayings, and also to Paul's desire to emphasise that the wine, as well as the bread, must be consumed reverently in memory of the Lord.[78] If the original report contained the saying twice, it is argued, it is unlikely that the symmetry would have been destroyed. The argument is not quite convincing here, since Schürmann holds that Luke's 'likewise' also contains a reference to the command to repeat the action; in other words, if the command is authentic, Schürmann wants to claim that it must have been given twice, that the Lucan account suppressed the second occurrence, and that the Pauline account restored it. The position would then be like that with the account of the distribution of the cup, where we saw that, if the Lucan/Pauline account is the oldest tradition, it nevertheless logically presupposes an account of the kind found in Mark. In short, it looks as though the earliest tradition reported such a command by Jesus with both the bread-word and the cup-word, in which case, whatever its relative age, the Pauline form is logically prior to the Lucan.

But now we must ask whether the command goes back to the earliest form of the sayings of Jesus. Schürmann makes two points here. First, he argues that it is historically probable that Jesus gave such a command, since without it we cannot explain why the early church continued to celebrate the rite. He argues that the rite itself indicates that Jesus wished his disciples to repeat it, and that the preservation of the narrative shows that this is how the early church understood the situation.[79] He also mentions briefly and dismisses the argument that Jesus expected the parousia so soon that he could not have envisaged the possibility of his disciples continuing to meet together to remember his death, and his criticism of this argument has been upheld by Patsch.[80] We can perhaps strengthen Schürmann's first point by two observations. First, if the Last Supper was a Passover meal, it is hard to see how the Lord's Supper came to be held not annually but much more frequently in the early church without some indication from Jesus himself. Second, if the decisive events that established the church were the resurrection appearances of Jesus and the outpouring of the Spirit, it is all the more remarkable that the early church celebrated his death in the Lord's Supper and made no explicit reference to his resurrection; could they have done so without a very firm conviction that Jesus had commanded them to remember his death in this way? A further point is that the command is originally a command to repeat the rite; the accent lies on 'Do this'. In Paul, however, the accent is more on remembering the Lord. It is arguable that this accent developed once the church had begun to keep the rite, and that the force of the command in the Lucan account is earlier.[81] In short, there is a good case that Jesus intended that his disciples should continue the rite, and that he explicitly commanded them to do so. M. Goguel's statement 'What is explicitly stated in Luke is implicit in Mark'[82] can, however, raise the question whether an explicit command was necessary and whether it is authentic.

Hence Schürmann's second point is concerned with the literary problem of the originality of the Lucan/Pauline account by comparison with that of Mark. On the one hand, there is no good reason to doubt that Jesus could have given a command of this nature. On the other hand, the question arises whether we can satisfactorily explain why Mark omitted it, if it was original. Jeremias is able to avoid this difficulty by claiming that the command, which he regards as authentic (admittedly on the basis of a dubious interpretation), was handed down in a different tradition from that known by Mark; he argues that the liturgical formula would not necessarily have contained a direction to repeat the action, since, in P. Benoit's words, 'On ne récite pas une rubrique, on l'exécute', and he makes the important point that what Jesus said at the Last Supper is not confined to what found its way into what we may call the official report.[83] This is a weak argument, since it is the less liturgically-formed text (Mark) which omits the rubric and the more liturgically-formed text (Paul) which includes it. One might more plausibly reverse Jeremias's argument and say that the liturgical text retained an element which was not incorporated in the narrative text in Mark since the latter is more an account of what Jesus did than a rubric for use in the church. This is in effect the position of Schürmann, although he adds other reasons which are less persuasive.[84] None of these arguments bear any weight for H. Patsch who holds that the tendency was to conservation rather than to deletion of dominical sayings, and that, if Jesus' intention that the rite should be repeated is implicit in Mark's account, it is strange if the explicit unfolding of this motif was dropped in the tradition.[85]

From this discussion it is clear that the one real argument against the authenticity of the saying is its absence from Mark. There is nothing in the content of the saying to suggest that it is inauthentic,[86] and indeed its Palestinian background points in the direction of authenticity. In view of this point it may well be dangerous to attach too much weight to the absence of the command from Mark. We have already seen that to talk of *the* original report of the Last Supper may be misleading, and hence it may not be necessary to look for specific reasons why the command was missing from the Marcan form of the tradition. Even, then, if we cannot be sure about the precise tradition-history of the command, we may claim that the arguments against its historicity are not conclusive, and that at the very least we may use the saying as a guide to the intention of Jesus at the Last Supper.

(5). *The sayings about the kingdom*

In Luke's account of the Last Supper the sayings about the bread and the cup are preceded by two other sayings of Jesus. In the first of them he expresses his great desire to eat the Passover with his disciples and then says that he will not eat it again until fulfilment comes in the kingdom of God. Then he takes a cup of wine, gives thanks in the usual way, and distributes it to the disciples with a similar remark that he will not drink of the fruit of the vine until the kingdom comes. Mark's account is different. Here there is only one saying, and it comes after the meal. Having spoken the cup-saying Jesus goes straight on to say that he will not drink again from the fruit of the vine until he drinks it new in the kingdom of God. There is nothing corresponding to this in Paul's account. However, Paul does close his account with the words that by eating and drinking they 'proclaim the Lord's death until he comes'.

We can be fairly certain that the phrase just cited from Paul is evidence that he knew the tradition contained in the Gospels; he has alluded to it but has brought it into relation with the Christian hope of the parousia of Jesus by referring to the coming of Jesus rather than of the kingdom.[87] Furthermore, it is easy to account for the replacement of the sayings by an allusion in Paul. The Pauline account is a liturgical formula which preserves those elements of the narrative of the Last Supper which were significant for the celebration of the Lord's Supper, and these sayings of Jesus were not a necessary part of the liturgical text. At the same time, the fact that Paul alludes to the sayings is an indication that they formed part of the tradition before him, and are not a later creation.

We have now to consider whether Mark or Luke contains the primitive version of the saying or sayings. It is improbable that Jesus uttered the Lucan sayings before the bread-saying and cup-saying and the Marcan saying thereafter, since the Marcan saying and the second Lucan saying are very close in wording. Our problem, therefore, is whether the Lucan form is derived from the Marcan, or vice versa. Both views have their defenders.

R. Pesch has recently defended the theory that Luke 22:15–18 can be explained as a Lucan creation.[88] He follows such earlier scholars as P. Benoit, W. G. Kümmel and J. Wanke[89] in arguing that Luke wished to stress the paschal character of the Last Supper and also to develop the thought of the betrayal and denial of Jesus in the conversation after the meal. It therefore suited his purpose to bring forward the content of Mark 14:25 to a place immediately before the meal and to rewrite that saying in the form of two parallel sayings. This claim is substantiated by the arguments that Luke 22:15–18 contains nothing that could not have been derived from Mark, and that its style is Lucan and contains no original Semitic features which might indicate that a primitive source was being used.

The opposing view is defended by J. Jeremias, H. Schürmann and H. Patsch.[90] It is presented most fully by Schürmann. He argues in general terms that Luke does not make transpositions in the order of material from his sources, that he does not create parallel formations, and that his tendency is to abbreviate Mark rather than to expand it. These points are broadly correct, although some exceptions to them can be found.[91] Next, a detailed linguistic examination of the section in Luke follows, in which it is argued that, although the passage contains clear signs of Lucan editing, it is not Mark which is being rewritten but a non-Marcan source, and that Mark's account was dependent on this hypothetical source. The reasoning here is not as convincing as in other parts of Schürmann's work, and he does not really demonstrate that Luke 22:15–18 is not a mosaic of Marcan phrases which Luke has used to create a new narrative. However, there are a number of places where the style of the passage is paralleled in other material peculiar to Luke rather than in passages where Luke is editing Marcan material; if it is correct that we can to some extent distinguish the style of Luke's non-Marcan material from his own style, there is some evidence here that the passage before us is not entirely the result of Luke's own editing of Mark.[92] A verdict on the matter must rest to some extent on a general impression regarding the degree of Lucan creativity elsewhere in the Gospel; it seems highly improbable to me that Luke would have created sayings of Jesus in the manner suggested by the theory that here he is dependent on Mark.

Schürmann further defends his view by arguing that Luke 22:15–18 is a self-contained unit, which was originally separate from vs. 19–20. The latter verses are a kind of appendix added to this account of the Passover meal held by Jesus in order to explain its eucharistic significance. On this view, it is one and the same cup which is mentioned in vs. 17 and 20. This account of the meal without eucharistic colouring is said to be attested in Mark 14:25, a saying which originally was preceded by an account of the meal similar to that in Luke 22:15–18; this account was removed when the liturgical unit in Mark 14:22–24 was inserted. Further, the same non-eucharistic meal-report lies behind John 13–17. The original account was concerned with Jesus' double-prophecy of his approaching death, and this was then turned into an account of Jesus' last Passover meal.

This particular part of Schürmann's theory is far from convincing. It depends on the view that the account of the institution of the Lord's Supper is a later addition to the text, and there is really no evidence to support this. Since the Passover setting runs through the accounts, it is unlikely that the Lucan tradition added this to the story, and one cannot really say that the Passover element has been underlined and developed in the present form of the story. Schürmann attaches some importance to 22:16 as indicating that Luke's account was formed against the background of a continuing Christian Passover celebration in the early church. But it is doubtful how far there was a distinctive Christian celebration of the Passover in the first century, although we have evidence for its existence in the second century, and it is even more doubtful how far any such annual celebration influenced the form of the narratives of the Last Supper.[93] Without going any more deeply into the details, we must be content to say that Schürmann's theory of a narrative of the Passover meal, which was later enlarged to give an account of the institution of the Lord's Supper, is unconvincing. It is more probable that from the beginning the story of the Last Supper was told in the context of its Jewish setting and as a pattern provided by Jesus for the church to follow.

So far, then, as the material in Luke 22:15–18/Mark 14:25 is concerned, we have seen that there is a reasonable case that Luke could have derived his material from a substantial revision of Mark, but that this process is not altogether probable. If the Lucan material is not derived from Mark, there remains the question whether the Marcan saying is dependent on Luke. Even Schürmann admits that the wording of Mark 14:25 appears to be more primitive than that of Luke, so that it is unlikely that the Marcan saying is based on the tradition preserved in Luke. Patsch argues that we have two branches of tradition; the Marcan tradition omitted the Passover saying, which was less relevant for the church, but preserved the Cup saying in its more primitive form.[94] This view fits in with the argument by Jeremias that Luke has preserved the sayings in their historical position before the words of institution.[95]

Once again, we find that, whichever form of the tradition is accepted as original, the essential theological content is not seriously affected. Both forms of the tradition record Jesus' affirmation that this would be his last meal with his disciples before the coming of the kingdom brings about a new situation. In short, although the examination of the texts has shown the difficulties in establishing the original wording of the report of Jesus' last meal, the essential content of what happened and what Jesus said is remarkably unaffected by this uncertainty. This does not mean that the examination was unnecessary; on the contrary, historical investigation of this kind is a necessary preliminary to a study of this story and has helped to show that the narrative is securely based in early and reliable tradition which has been preserved in more than one line of transmission.

CHAPTER THREE

What Kind of Meal was the Last Supper?

In all three of the synoptic Gospels we are told that the Last
Supper of Jesus was a Passover meal. The meal which the disciples were sent to prepare is clearly stated to be the Passover
(Mark 14:12–16; Luke 22:7–13), and Jesus then acted as host
at this meal with his disciples. Consequently, at first sight there
would seem to be nothing that requires extended discussion in
this chapter. Unfortunately, things are seldom as simple as they
seem, and there are a number of objections to the view which
we have just stated. The principal objection is that if we turn to
the Gospel of John we shall find evidence that the Jews had not
yet celebrated the Passover at the time when Jesus had already
concluded his meal and was on trial before Pilate (John 18:28).
In fact John states that the day of the crucifixion was the Day
of Preparation of the Passover (John 19:24); *i.e.* this is often
taken to mean that after Jesus died in the afternoon the setting
of the sun marked the beginning of the feast day which commenced with the celebration of the Passover meal; in line with
this chronology John 13:1 would suggest that the meal held by
Jesus took place 'before the feast of the Passover'. In short, it
appears that John follows a different chronology from that in
the Synoptic Gospels (see Table 4). We need to investigate more

closely to find out exactly what was happening and whether there is any way in which the Gospel accounts can be brought into harmony with one another.

PASCHAL FEATURES IN THE LAST SUPPER

Our first step must be to take note of any features which confirm or even prove that the Last Supper was a Passover meal. The evidence which can be brought forward may be of various kinds. First, there is evidence which is consistent with the paschal character of the meal, although it is not sufficient by itself to prove the fact. Second, there is evidence which may suggest that the meal can only have been a paschal meal. Third, since the Synoptic accounts were written on the assumption that the meal was a Passover meal, it is arguable that they deliberately introduced paschal features into the account. It is worth asking, therefore, if there are any pieces of evidence which resist attempts to explain them away as details invented by the Evangelists. Fourth, since it is John's Gospel which gives the impression that Jesus' meal was not a Passover meal, it is worth asking whether this Gospel contains any evidence that supports the paschal character of the meal.

One important point should be made at the outset. So long as it is claimed that the actual account of the institution of the Lord's Supper (Mark 14:22–24; Luke 22:19–20; 1 Cor. 11:23–25) is a self-contained unit which has been placed in its present setting in the Gospels, it is possible to claim that the setting may be secondary and unhistorical. Scholars who adopt this position argue that we must demonstrate the presence of paschal features in the account of the institution and not just in the surrounding narrative.[1] This is an exacting demand to meet, since the account of the words of institution is concerned with the limited purpose of establishing what Jesus did that was significant for the church's meal and assumes that the readers are aware of the original setting. The absence of paschal features from this section, therefore, is not necessarily an argument against the paschal setting of the meal. However, we have already argued that the words of institution should not be regarded as a separable piece of older tradition but as forming an integral part of the Last Supper narrative as a whole.[2]

The features of the narrative which suggest that a Passover meal was being held have been listed and examined in detail by

J. Jeremias, and there is little that can be added to his magisterial treatment.[3] What follows is heavily dependent on his work.

(1). The Synoptic Gospels specifically date the meal on the Day of Passover. Mark 14:12 tells us that the disciples made their preparations for the meal 'on the first day of Unleavened Bread, when they sacrificed the passover lamb'.[4] If the meal was not a Passover meal, it follows that this statement must be either a historical error or that it needs some kind of reinterpretation.

(2). The meal was held in Jerusalem. The force of this observation lies in the fact that at this time Jesus and his disciples were staying outside Jerusalem at Bethany, and returning there each night. One would have expected them to return to their lodging for their evening meal. But the Passover lamb could be eaten only in Jerusalem itself, despite the great crowds and the consequent pressure on the available accommodation.

(3). The meal was held in the evening (Mark 14:17; John 13:30; 1 Cor. 11:23). The normal mealtimes for the Jews were in the morning and the afternoon. On a special occasion, it is true, a meal might last beyond sunset into the evening. In the case of the Passover, however, the meal was eaten in the evening and not earlier.

(4). Jeremias argues that Jesus usually ate with large numbers of his disciples and hearers. On this occasion, however, he is specifically said to have gathered with the Twelve, a number which corresponds with the requirement that the Passover should be celebrated in groups of at least ten persons. It is arguable that Jesus deliberately limited his companions to the usual size of a Passover group. However, this particular point cannot be regarded as a compelling one since we have no proof whatever that Jesus usually ate with a larger company of people, and also since it is possible that some of the women associated with the followers of Jesus were present at the last meal.

(5). The guests are specifically said to have reclined at the meal (Mark 14:18; John 13:22, 28). To recline was a mark of freedom and was therefore customary at the Passover. Otherwise, sitting was the normal posture at meals. However, it should be noted that reclining was a feature of festive meals in general and was not confined to the Passover meal.

(6). Jeremias argues from John 13:10 that the guests were in a state of levitical purity such as was required for the eating of the passover lamb. This seems, however, to be a somewhat precarious deduction from the text, and it should be received with considerable caution.[5]

(7). Both Mark and Luke place the eating of bread by Jesus and the disciples in the middle of the meal and not at the beginning. This was unusual, and it corresponds with the order of the Passover meal which has been described earlier.[6] If Mark's order is to be trusted, the guests had already partaken of a dish of food before the bread was distributed (Mark 14:20). Two points remain uncertain. The first is that the order of the saying about the dish (Mark 14:20) and the distribution of the bread (Mark 14:22) is reversed in Luke 22:19f., 21–23.[7] If the Lucan order is correct, however, it is still the case that both Mark and Luke do not place the distribution of the bread at the beginning of the meal. The second point, which is much weightier, is that at a formal Jewish guest meal, the guests were served with a preliminary course in an adjacent room before proceeding to the dining room to commence the meal proper; we may compare the modern custom of serving drinks to guests in one room before taking seats for dinner in another.[8] Jeremias states that such a preliminary course in an anteroom can hardly account for Mark's language here. If, however, we regard the formality of the description in our sources as being typical of a wealthy household in later times, it is possible that in the first century a guest meal could begin with hors d'oeuvres and give rise to the kind of description here in Mark. In short, the possibility that Mark is describing a guest meal, such as might be held on any special occasion, cannot perhaps be altogether excluded,[9] although it must be insisted that Mark clearly intends the description to be that of a Passover meal.

(8). The drinking of wine was not customary at ordinary meals, but was normal at festal meals and required at the Passover. Wine was also drunk at the ceremony of sanctifying the Sabbath. Hence the use of wine by Jesus is consistent with a Passover meal but not peculiar to this occasion. Jeremias further argues that Jesus used red wine to signify his blood. Red wine was a requirement at the Passover meal, although of course it was also served on other occasions. This point, then, would help to confirm that a Passover meal is being described. One possible weakness in the argument is that Jesus could have used another colour of wine to signify his blood if the point of comparison was its fluidity rather than its colour.

(9). During the meal Judas went out, and the disciples thought that he was going to buy something for the feast or to give something to the poor (John 13:29). Jeremias argues that a hasty visit to make purchases was unlikely on the day before the feast (since the whole of the next day would be available for purchases) but would make good sense at a Passover meal because for the next two days no purchases would be possible. He also claims that giving something to the poor was customary on Passover night. The attempt to dismiss this argument on the grounds that the verse in question is a literary device by the Evangelist is quite unconvincing;[10] even a literary device would have to be convincing to the readers.

(10). Mark tells us that the meal ended with singing. This refers to the second part of the Passover *hallel*. There seems to be no evidence for a similar occurrence at the end of any other kind of Jewish meal. If the meal was not the Passover, either Mark has continued to describe it mistakenly as though it were, or it is argued, the description could be based on early Christian practice in concluding the Lord's Supper with a hymn.[11] Neither of these suggestions carries any weight.

(11). After the meal Jesus stayed close to Jerusalem and did not return to Bethany, since the night of the Passover had to be spent in Jerusalem or its immediate neighbourhood. It could be that other reasons determined Jesus' decision to stay in the area of Jerusalem; possibly he did not wish to go as far as Bethany so late at night. Nevertheless, his behaviour certainly fitted in with the ritual requirements.

(12). Jeremias attaches supreme importance to the fact that Jesus interpreted the significance of the bread and wine to the disciples at the meal and argues that Jesus was following the normal practice at the Passover meal. The words of interpretation correspond not to the prayers of thanksgiving for the bread and wine, which Jesus offered as a matter of course, but to the Passover *haggadah* which brought out the symbolical significance of the various parts of the meal and did so with reference to the past redemptive act of God at the Exodus and the hope of his future grace to Israel. The objection raised by E. Schweizer to this argument is that 'the words of interpretation do not correspond to those spoken at the Passover, where for instance the particular meaning of the unleavened bread is expounded.'[12] But this objection is surely beside the mark, since one would expect Jesus to give the elements a new interpretation. Jeremias himself deals with the possible objection that Jesus' interpretation came at a different point in the meal from the *haggadah* by claiming that Jesus wished to combine his new interpretation with the distribution of the elements.

We have now listed the twelve arguments adduced for

identifying the Last Supper as the Passover meal. We have seen
that arguments (4), (5), (6) and (8) confirm the paschal character
of the meal but could apply to a festal meal. Argument (1) is a clear
statement of the Evangelists' interpretation of the meal, and
arguments (2), (3), (7), (9), (10), (11) and (12) refer fairly specifically to the requirements of a Passover meal. Of these arguments,
numbers (2), (3), (4), (5), (6), (9) and (11) are confirmed by the
evidence in the Gospel of John, and four of these points are
among the stronger pieces of evidence for regarding the Last
Supper as a paschal meal. Opinions will differ as to how far the
Evangelists could be regarded as deliberately describing what
was not a paschal meal as though it was such a meal, and how
far they are incorporating traditional material which witnesses
directly or indirectly to the nature of the occasion. In our opinion
points (3), (7), (9), (10) and (12) offer the evidence on which most
weight can be placed, and it should be observed that point (12)
belongs to the central core of the tradition about the meal. It may
well be claimed that from the beginning the tradition indirectly
and perhaps directly testified that the meal had a paschal character. The *prima facie* impression which we get from the Synoptic
Gospels is thus confirmed when we dig below the surface of the
narrative.

DIFFICULTIES WITH THE PASCHAL SETTING OF THE MEAL

We have already seen that John's Gospel appears to conflict with
the clear testimony of the Synoptic Gospels and the tradition
which they enshrine. But before we look more closely at the
problems which it raises we must ask whether there are any
other difficulties in the way of accepting the presentation of the
character of the meal in the Synoptic Gospels. There is indeed a
formidable case against the picture so far presented, and again
we are indebted to Jeremias for a comprehensive assembling and
discussion of no less than ten objections (apart from the problems raised by John).[13] There is not much to be added to his
discussion, but since some of the objections may still seem to
be cogent despite his comments on them we need to go over the
ground once again.

(1). We can ignore the objection by J. Wellhausen that Mark
14:22 speaks of 'bread' rather than of 'unleavened bread' and
therefore cannot refer to the Passover. There is abundant evidence that 'bread' *simpliciter* can mean unleavened bread.

(2). It has been argued that since the early church celebrated a meal daily (Acts 2:42, 46), this cannot have been derived from the example of a yearly Passover meal. But what Jesus told the disciples to repeat was not the Passover meal but a particular ritual within that meal. Moreover, the daily gathering of the disciples to eat together was natural in view of their daily gathering together with Jesus during his lifetime.

(3). It has been objected that there is no reference to the Passover lamb and the bitter herbs in the account in Mark. This, however, is not surprising in an account which concentrates on the parts of the meal which were significant for the Lord's Supper. In any case, the dish of bitter herbs may well be meant in Mark 14:20 and the Passover Lamb is mentioned in Mark 14:12 and Luke 22:15. The objection, therefore, is not cogent. Nevertheless, Mark's silence about the lamb in the words of institution may well imply that Jesus is unlikely to have compared himself directly with it in the same way as he reinterpreted the bread and the cup.[14]

(4). It has been maintained (a). that at the Passover the bread was broken first and then the blessing was said, contrary to Mark 14:22; (b). that individual cups were used rather than a common cup; and (c). that each guest had his own dish of bitter herbs (contrast Mark 14:20). The first of these points appears to rest on an erroneous interpretation of late Jewish sources. The third point appears to rest on late Jewish custom. The second point is controversial. According to Jeremias the practice of individual cups dates from the second century and replaced the earlier custom of having one cup for all.[15] However, the opposite position is adopted by H. Schürmann, who argues that Jesus deliberately went against the normal custom of having individual cups by inviting the disciples to share his cup.[16] The rabbinic evidence on this point is difficult to evaluate. We know that in the second century the use of individual cups was normal and that the use of a single cup was also found. But it seems impossible to conclude with any certainty what the practice in the first century was. We certainly cannot say that the practice of Jesus rules out the possibility that this was a Passover meal, especially since the same practice may have been followed at the Passover as at an ordinary guest meal. In any case, it is possible that Jesus deliberately adopted a special way of distributing the wine in order to draw an unusual lesson from it.[17]

(5). According to Mark 14:2 the Sanhedrin resolved not to arrest Jesus 'during the feast' in order to avoid a disturbance;

if they kept to their intention, then the arrest of Jesus immediately after the meal must have taken place before the feast.
The objection that the Sanhedrin may have changed its mind
is a weak one, since on this view it is difficult to see why Mark
recorded an unfulfilled intention. Much the better reply is that
the crucial phrase should be translated 'in the presence of the
festal crowd' (*cf.* Luke 22:6, 'in the absence of the multitude').[18]
The Sanhedrin wanted to arrest Jesus quietly when the crowds
of his supporters were not around, and Judas's treachery enabled
them to do precisely this.

(6). The release of Barabbas by Pilate as an amnesty in connection with the Passover (Mark 15:6) has been understood in
the light of a rabbinic rule that 'They may slaughter (*sc.* the Passover lamb) ... for one whom they have promised to bring out
of prison' (Pesahim 8:6).[19] If the release of Barabbas followed
this rule, then it would appear that he was released *before* the
Passover meal, and this would contradict the synoptic chronology of the meal. Jeremias avoids the difficulty by arguing that
the Jewish regulation has nothing to do with Pilate's action, since
the former deals with a promise of freedom by the Jewish authorities. But it is by no means impossible that a reference to
Roman imprisonment is included. The chronological problem
may be solved by arguing that Pilate acted too late in this instance
for the released prisoner to be able to take part in the Passover.[20]
Nevertheless, it should be observed that here we may well have
a clash between the picture of events in the synoptic Gospels
and the official Jewish calendar.

(7). According to 1 Corinthians 5:7 Paul refers to the death
of Jesus as 'our paschal lamb'. It can be argued that this allusion
requires that Jesus was put to death at the same time as the
paschal lambs were slaughtered at the temple, namely on the
afternoon of Nisan 14 before the Passover meal was eaten. To
argue thus, however, is surely to press the allusion too far,
although of course it would be consistent with the death of Jesus
on Nisan 14 if this received independent substantiation.

(8). Another passage in 1 Corinthians (15:20) refers to Jesus
as 'the first fruits of those who have fallen asleep.' The early
Christians celebrated Sunday as the day of his resurrection. Now
since the idea of first fruits is derived from the Jewish practice
of the dedication of the first fruits of the harvest on 'the morrow
after the sabbath' (Lv. 23:9–14), it can be argued that the resurrection of Jesus took place on Nisan 16, and that therefore he
was crucified on Nisan 14, the day before the Passover meal.[21]

This would fit in with the chronological argument based on 1 Corinthians 5:7, but again it must be emphasised, and all the more strongly in this case, that Paul is not making a chronological statement.[22]

(9). It used to be argued that the ritual practices of the early Christian sect known as the Quartodecimans were based on the view that Jesus died on Nisan 14; this sect, it was held, used to fast until the afternoon of Nisan 14, the point at which Jesus was thought to have died, and then they celebrated the Lord's Supper. More recent study has shown that in fact the Quartodecimans fasted until the middle of the night of Nisan 14/15 and then held their meal; consequently their practice has no relevance for the chronology of the Last Supper.[23]

(10). Finally, there is a set of objections which are concerned not with the Last Supper itself but with the following events. It is argued that numerous details in the account of the trial and crucifixion of Jesus are inconsistent with the fact that this was the Passover day, which was celebrated as a Sabbath. Several of these objections are quite lacking in force and can be ignored.[24] The more important ones must be mentioned. First of all, there is the fact that the Sanhedrin met to try and condemn Jesus on the day of the Passover feast. Criminal trials were undoubtedly not permitted on feast days, but equally they were not permitted on the day preceding a festival.[25] Hence, even if we adopt the view that Jesus was executed on the day preceding the Passover, we are still faced with this difficulty. In other words, this particular objection is a difficulty for any chronology of the Last Supper and death of Jesus and not for the synoptic representation of events only. The solution to the difficulty will lie in the fact that the Jewish authorities took special measures to deal with what they regarded as an unusual case; the actual conduct of the trial was somewhat irregular, and we need not be surprised if the timing of it was also irregular. Jeremias further argues that since false prophets were to be executed in the presence of all the people, it would be necessary to put Jesus to death during the festival before the crowds had departed from Jerusalem.

Second, there is the trial of Jesus and his execution by the Romans on the feast day. Here it can be argued that the Romans were not bound by Jewish law and could act as they pleased. Nevertheless, one can argue that they would have been unlikely to risk flouting Jewish opinion by desecrating a feast day. In particular, it is significant that the Romans proceeded to execute the two criminals along with Jesus, although presumably there was no urgent necessity to put them to death. This may well appear to be the strongest objection to the chronology of the Last Supper as a Passover meal. Yet it must again be observed that the objections to an execution on the Day of the Passover apply almost as strongly to an execution on the preceding day when the lambs were being ritually slaughtered at the temple. In any case, we have some evidence for executions taking place on the Sabbath, and it is arguable that the Romans, perhaps under Jewish official pressure, were prepared to use the crucifixion of Jesus and the other criminals as a public example when large crowds were gathered in Jerusalem. It must be concluded that we are dealing with an unprecedented event which is quite conceivable given the unusual situation.

Third, it has been argued that the burial of Jesus and the accompanying purchases could not have taken place on the evening of the Day of Passover, which was the weekly Sabbath. Since, however, early burial was necessary in general, and since the body of an executed criminal could not be left hanging overnight the law certainly permitted exceptions to be made to the usual Sabbath restrictions.

The effect of this discussion is to show that several of the objections to dating the events following the Last Supper on the Day of the Passover still apply if we place the events twenty-four hours later, and that all the objections can be adequately refuted, provided that we make the reasonable assumption that the Jewish authorities acted irregularly over the trial of Jesus. Admittedly not all scholars find the case persuasive. R.E. Brown replies to Jeremias by commenting: 'However, so much activity on a feast remains a difficulty; and it seems more plausible to accept John's chronology whereby such activity takes place on an ordinary day, not a holyday'.[26] The weakness of this view is that the difficulties are not significantly reduced by placing everything a day earlier, as appears to be the case in John. It emerges that the chronological problem cannot be settled primarily by considering the weight of the historical objections to the synoptic presentation of the course of events. We need to look again at the presentation in John.

THE PROBLEMS RAISED BY THE GOSPEL OF JOHN

Although the meal described in John 13 lacks the particular features which characterise the synoptic accounts of the Last Supper, there can be no doubt that John intends to describe the same meal; this is evident from the prophecy of the betrayal by Judas which occurs during the meal and from the position of the meal in relation to the arrest in the garden. We shall have to consider the theological significance of John's account of the meal later. At present our concern is with the general chronological structure of John. We have already seen that there are a number of indications that John regarded this meal as occurring twenty-four hours earlier than the appointed time for the Passover meal. How are we to deal with this problem? Essentially three types of solution have been offered. (1). There is the view that the dating of the meal in John is historically correct. If we accept this view, we must explain how the synoptic Gospels have presented a misleading picture, and also suggest what kind of meal Jesus was holding with his disciples if it was not a Passover meal. (2). The converse of the first view is that the dating in the synoptic Gospels is correct. If so, either John is historically in error on the matter, or else the evidence which suggests the earlier date for the meal can be interpreted in a different manner. (3). There is, however, a third possibility which is that both accounts are correct, and that the differences between them arise from different ways of reckoning the date of the Passover festival. Each of these views has its supporters, and we must examine them in turn.

(1). *The Johannine chronology*

The view that John is correct and the synoptic Gospels are mistaken has commanded considerable support.[27] Those who adopt it claim as a principal argument in its favour that it removes many of the historical objections to the synoptic dating. We have already seen, however, that some of the same difficulties exist for the Johannine dating. Adoption of the Johannine dating does not greatly alter the situation. Further, this view necessitates the hypothesis that the paschal representation of the Last Supper in the synoptic Gospels is late and unhistorical. But again we have seen that the paschal features are many and some of them are firmly tied into the narrative. If we nevertheless continue to maintain this view, we must ask what kind of meal Jesus was holding. The simplest answer is that Jesus was holding a somewhat formal guest meal with his disciples, which would have followed a basically similar pattern to the Passover meal.

At a guest meal the participants commenced with a preliminary course served, at least in later times, in an ante-room, and consisting of wine, for which each guest said his own thanks, and hors d'oeuvres. When the guests reclined at the table, the host gave thanks for the bread, broke it and distributed it to the guests, who used pieces of it to convey the main course to their mouths (just as we might eat beans or cheese on toast). During the meal the host gave thanks for the wine when it was first served. After the main course there was a dessert, and finally, after the guests had washed their hands, one of the guests took the 'cup of blessing' and gave thanks for it.[28]

It is obviously not impossible that Jesus was holding this kind of meal, although we must then ask how it came to be transformed into an explicitly paschal meal in the tradition. We are also left with the task of explaining how Jesus was able to use the food in the meal to provide the basis for the words of institution in the same general kind of way as took place in a paschal meal.

This last remark leads us to the second possibility which is that Jesus held a private and irregular paschal meal with his disciples twenty-four hours ahead of the proper time. This view has been adopted by a number of scholars including V. Taylor and F. F. Bruce.[29] If this view is accepted, it is doubtful whether the meal included a Passover lamb, since presumably the priests would not have accepted a sacrifice before the official time. After AD 70 when the temple no longer stood the Passover had to be celebrated without the sacrifice of a lamb. The important question is whether this practice existed before AD 70. Although there is some evidence for the slaughter of paschal lambs outside Jerusalem before AD 70, it seems probable on the whole that, if the Passover was celebrated away from Jerusalem, there was no slaughter of a paschal lamb and a meal of unleavened bread had to suffice. It is possible that the same practice was followed in Palestine, particularly by any groups that did not accept the temple and its worship.[30]

If this view is adopted, we are again faced with the question of how the synoptic Gospels came to date the Last Supper on the proper day of the Jewish calendar for the Passover. We shall return to this point, but first of all we must look at the second possible answer to the problem of dating, namely that the statements in John can be harmonised with those in the synoptic Gospels.

(2). *The synoptic chronology*

The view that the Johannine evidence can be reinterpreted to bring it into line with the synoptic Gospels has been argued by

J. Jeremias, who does not claim to be more than partially successful, and also by J. N. Geldenhuys, who attempts a complete solution to the problem.[31] We have already seen that there are some phrases in John which are consistent with the synoptic dating of the meal. There are others which appear to contradict it. The first of these is John 13:1–4 which is translated in the RSV: 'Now before the feast of the Passover, when Jesus knew that his hour had come to depart out of this world to the Father, having loved his own who were in the world, he loved them to the end. And during supper, when the devil had already put it into the heart of Judas Iscariot, Simon's son, to betray him, Jesus ... rose from supper.' At first sight this text suggests that the supper was held 'before the feast of the Passover'. However, a number of scholars have argued that the time-phrase goes with the phrase 'when Jesus knew' rather than with the main clause of the sentence, and that consequently the date of the supper is left undetermined.[32] We would then have a contrast between the knowledge of Jesus before the feast that his hour had come, and the continuation of his love for his disciples right through to the bitter end at the time of the feast. Other scholars regard the emphatic time-phrase at the beginning of the sentence as providing the temporal setting for the great act of love which Jesus showed.[33] This seems to be the more likely understanding of the sentence. The former view assumes that 'when Jesus knew' refers to a time before the time of the main verb, but in fact the phrase more probably refers to the same time as the main verb (*cf.* John 13:3) and suggests that the great act of love took place before the Passover.

The second passage in John is 18:28 which states that on the morning of the crucifixion the Jews were unwilling to enter the praetorium 'so that they might not be defiled, but might eat the passover'. This verse reflects the Jewish fear of contracting uncleanness through entry into a Gentile house and so being ritually prevented from taking part in the Passover.[34] An attempt to harmonise the verse with the synoptic chronology has been made by arguing that 'the passover' here means the daily sacrifice offered during the period of the festival and especially on Nisan 15.[35] It is doubtful whether John's readers would have recognised this meaning for the phrase. P. Billerbeck argues that this meaning was possible only in a context which demanded it, and holds that this is not the case here, especially if the Gospel was written for Gentile readers without a precise knowledge of Jewish customs.[36] Geldenhuys holds that readers familiar with the tradition that Jesus was slain on the Day of the Passover would have recognised that the phrase was being used in its less usual meaning.[37] It is, however, far from certain that John's readers knew the other Gospels in detail; if the Gospel had an evangelistic purpose, it is indeed highly unlikely that some of the readers would have known the other Gospels. Consequently, this point must remain doubtful. A further difficulty, which L. Morris regards as quite decisive, is that the phrase 'to eat the Passover' refers in the sources to eating the Passover lamb *and* the other offerings of the feast, and not to eating the latter without the former.[38]

Third, John describes the day of the crucifixion as the day of Preparation of the Passover (19:14). This is usually taken to refer to Nisan 14, the day for preparing the feast to be eaten on Nisan 15. Hence Jesus would have been crucified on the same day as the lambs were being slaughtered for the Passover meal. However, the day before the Sabbath was also known as the day of Preparation, and it is linguistically possible that John's phrase should be taken to mean 'the day of Preparation for the Sabbath which fell during the Passover'.[39] Since we know from the other Gospels that Jesus was crucified on the day of Preparation for the Sabbath (Mark 14:42), and since John himself explicitly refers to the day of Preparation as being the day before the Sabbath (19:31, *cf*. 42), it is very likely that he was thinking of the same day in 19:14. Further, the actual phrase 'the day of Preparation for the Passover' as a way of referring to Nisan 14 is otherwise unattested, both in Aramaic and in Greek.[40] There is thus a good case that John's phrase means 'Friday', and the attempt to discredit this view by saying that it serves to harmonise John and the synoptic Gospels[41] carries no conviction. However, it must be observed that John's usage at this point can support either the synoptic chronology or his own *prima facie* chronology, since all the Gospels agree that Jesus died on a Friday.

Our discussion of the evidence has shown that of the three points where John is said to support a different chronology from the synoptic Gospels, the first is ambiguous but on the whole is strong, the second can hardly be explained away, and the third is irrelevant. An easy harmonisation of John with the synoptic chronology is not possible.[42] However, this does not entitle us to fly to the opposite extreme and argue that John (or his source) has consciously and deliberately altered the synoptic chronology in the interests of his own theology.[43] This theory is not upheld by the evidence.

(3). *Chronological harmonisation*

We come, therefore, to the third type of theory which argues that both John and the synoptic Gospels are right, and the differences between them are due to their describing the same events from different chronological points of view. Various different ways of explaining the differences in this way have been suggested.

(a). Historically one of the earliest explanations is that of J. Calvin who recognised that 'no clever device can get round the fact that on the day on which they crucified Christ they did not hold the festival (on which it would have been forbidden to hold an execution) but on that day held their normal preparation, and proceeded to eat the Passover after the burial of Christ.' He argued that when a festival fell on the day before a Sabbath, the Jews postponed the festival to the Sabbath 'because two days on end without work would have seemed too difficult for the people'.[44] Jesus, therefore, held his meal at the proper time, but the Jewish official calendar placed the meal a day later. Unfortunately, there does not seem to be any evidence for the proposed postponement of a feast when it would have fallen on the day before the Sabbath.

(b). A second type of solution proposed by J. Pickl is that the number of lambs was too great to be slain on one day, and therefore the slaughter began on Nisan 13 when the Galileans sacrificed their lambs, while the Judeans waited until Nisan 14.[45] As in the case of the previous theory, there does not seem to be any evidence to support this suggestion.[46]

(c). Third, D. Chwolson proposed that the lambs were slaughtered in the evening between Nisan 14 and 15; when Nisan 15 fell on a Sabbath, the slaughter was brought forward twenty-four hours to the previous evening. Jesus, along with the Pharisees, could thus celebrate the meal on Nisan 14, while the Sadducees kept their lambs for twenty-four hours and then held the meal on Nisan 15.[47] This ingenious theory breaks down on various facts, the principal of which is that in the time of Jesus the Passover lambs were slain not in the evening between Nisan 14 and 15 but in the afternoon of Nisan 14.[48]

(d). An important variant of this theory was developed by P. Billerbeck. He argued that if the Passover was eaten on two different days in the year of the crucifixion, this means that two different groups of Jews were counting the days of the month differently. One group regarded Nisan 15 as beginning on Thursday evening, and the other group on Friday evening. Such a disparity was possible because it was the Jewish custom to insert extra days at the end of certain months in order to keep the lunar calendar of months in harmony with the solar calendar of years. People could make mistakes about the number of days intercalated. Further, the beginning of the new month was determined by observation of the new moon, which is a difficult procedure, and different observers could be a day out in their reckoning if, for example, there was fog. Billerbeck asked if there were any circumstances which could have led to the existence of two calendars a day out of step with each other in the year of the Last Supper. He noted that there was a group of Sadducees who reckoned that the offering of first fruits must take place on the day after the Sabbath that fell during the feast of Unleavened Bread, *i.e.* on a Sunday. This was based on their interpretation of Leviticus 23:11, 'the morrow after the sabbath'. But the Pharisees took the same phrase to refer to the day after the feast of the Passover, which was observed as a Sabbath. Thus for the Sadducees the offering always took place on a Sunday, and for the Pharisees always on Nisan 16. This divergence led to a corresponding divergence regarding the date of the feast of Pentecost, 50 days later. We know that the Pharisaic practice was followed in the first century, and that the Sadducees tried to oppose it. The argument is, then, that when circumstances were favourable the Sadducees tried to 'fix' the calendar so that the offering of first fruits would fall on a Sunday. If it looked as though Nisan 15 was going to be a Friday, they needed only to delay the beginning of the month by one day in order to make Nisan 15 a Saturday, and Nisan 16 a Sunday. If Nisan 15 was likely to be a Sunday, the beginning of the month could be advanced by one day to achieve the same result. We have evidence for the Sadducean group known as the Boethusians fiddling the beginning of the month for this purpose. Billerbeck argues that they tried to do so in the year in question, so that the Sadducees let Nisan 15 fall on a Saturday while the Pharisees insisted that Nisan 15 was the Friday. In order to avoid conflict the Sadducees, who controlled the temple, allowed the Pharisees to slaughter their Passover lambs one day early. Jesus followed the Pharisaic calendar and practice, and the synoptic Gospels report the Last Supper from this point of view, while the priests followed the Sadducean calendar, and John reports events from their point of view.[49]

Such is the theory, and Jeremias comments: 'This theory has been so thoroughly and carefully argued, especially by Billerbeck, that its possibility has to be admitted. Its weakness is that it is wholly conjectural; there is no evidence that the passover lambs were ever slaughtered on two consecutive days in the Temple, and it seems most unlikely that such a thing could ever have happened.'[50]

(e). A novel theory of the same general kind was developed by A. Jaubert. She demonstrated that, while the official Jewish calendar was, as we have just seen, a lunar calendar, there was also a solar calendar of 364 days, divided into four quarters of 91 days or 13 weeks. Adoption of this calendar meant that each quarter of the year began on the same day (a Wednesday) and thus the Jewish festivals always fell on the same day of the week. Hence the Passover meal would always be on a Tuesday evening. Now there is an early Christian document, the Syriac Didascalia, which offers a chronology of the passion in which Jesus held the Last Supper on Tuesday, was arrested the same night, and after his various trials was crucified on the Friday. Here, then, is a new solution of the problem. Jesus, it is held, followed the solar calendar, which was in use at Qumran and in the circles which produced the book of Jubilees, and held his Passover meal on a Tuesday evening, which was Nisan 15 by the solar calendar; but the priests did not hold their Passover meal until the Friday evening after he had died, which was Nisan 15 by the official, lunar calendar. If this view is adopted, we have to allow that the various trials of Jesus were spread over two or more days rather than being compressed into one night, as the Gospels appear to suggest, but at the same time there is the advantage that the very tight timetable in the Gospels becomes historically more credible.[51]

This ingenious theory has attracted a number of supporters,[52] but it has some weaknesses. First, it is doubtful whether we can deduce any historical information from the Syriac Didascalia, which was composed some 200 years after the death of Jesus. However, this objection is by no means as fatal as Jeremias supposes,[53] since the real question is about the possibility that Jesus could have followed the sectarian calendar. This leads to the second difficulty which is much more important. We have no other evidence to suggest that Jesus accepted any of the views of the Qumran sect, and adoption by him of their calendar would seem to be idiosyncratic. Nevertheless, it cannot be pronounced altogether impossible.[54] Third, on this view it is unlikely that Jesus celebrated his meal with a lamb, since we can hardly imagine the priesthood allowing ritual slaughter three days early to a group who were bitterly opposed to the temple and its staff. A fourth objection, which can be raised to other forms of the view that Jesus anticipated the official date of the Passover, is that such an act was illegal and therefore unlikely for Jesus; if, however, an earlier celebration was the practice among some more orthodox Jewish groups, this would make a deviation from the official timetable by Jesus somewhat more probable.

(f). Finally, in this catalogue of different calendars we come to a still more recent theory which has been presented particularly by H. Hoehner.[55] This view assumes the existence of two different ways of calculating the hours of the day. One way was the sunset-to-sunset reckoning of the day, which we have assumed in our discussion so far. The other method was from sunrise to sunrise. Both types of reckoning were used in the Bible. The theory now is that the people in Judaea, including the Sadducees, used the sunset-to-sunset reckoning, while the people in Galilee and the Pharisees used the sunrise-to-sunrise method. If so, Jesus, being a Galilean, slew his lamb on the Thursday afternoon which was Nisan 14, and held his meal in the evening of the same day, which was still Nisan 14 by the Galilean reckoning. For the Judaeans, however, Nisan 14 began at sunset, just before Jesus held his Supper, and so they slew their lambs the following afternoon (Friday) and ate their Passover supper on Friday evening, which was Nisan 15. This theory would require, as Hoehner recognises, two consecutive days of Passover sacrifices, but he reckons that this could have been possible in order to keep peace with the Pharisees. In other words, this theory faces the same difficulty as those of Pickl and Billerbeck. A second difficulty is that there is no explicit evidence for the two groups adopting two different methods of reckoning the day. However, there is a third objection, which seems fatal to me, namely that on this view the Galileans and Pharisees celebrated their Passover on Nisan 14, and not on Nisan 15, by their own reckoning, and this seems most unlikely.[56]

After this review of theories where do we stand? We have seen that there is an element of conjecture in all of the theories, but that some of them cannot be pronounced impossible. Billerbeck's theory is the most plausible. Since we have seen that both the synoptic Gospels and John contain clear evidence for their repective points of view, and since there is no reason to regard either of them as being mistaken, it seems best to adopt a solution of the third type, and to allow that the synoptic Gospels and John reflect the use of different calendars. The simple view that

Jesus held a meal twenty-four hours ahead of the official time founders on the explicit paschal chronology of the meal given in the synoptic Gospels; it is more probable that they are using a different paschal chronology from John.

Our conclusion, then, is that Jesus held a Passover meal earlier than the official Jewish date, and that he was able to do so as the result of calendar differences among the Jews.

CHAPTER FOUR

The Significance of the Last Supper

In the preceding sections we have attempted to show that the Last Supper held by Jesus with his disciples was a Passover meal, probably held in advance of the official date, which is to be understood against the background of the ideas associated with the Passover by the Jews. Our next task, therefore, is to see what happened at this meal and what significance Jesus attached to it.

JESUS AND THE LAST SUPPER

(1). *The Passover meal*

According to the synoptic Gospels Jesus celebrated his last meal as a Passover meal. On the appropriate day, by whatever calendar he was following, Jesus responded to the question of his disciples regarding where they should prepare for the meal by sending two of them to make the necessary arrangements in Jerusalem. The account of how the disciples were to follow a man carrying a jar of water suggests that a secret arrangement had already been made by Jesus rather than that he was exercising prophetic foreknowledge of what was going to happen.[1] Since the Gospels have already recorded the plot of the Jewish leaders to execute Jesus and the offer made by Judas to betray Jesus, it is probable that Jesus is regarded as having some knowledge of his dangerous situation and taking steps to avoid arrest before he was ready for it. All this suggests that Jesus, knowing of his imminent danger, attached a particular importance to this Passover meal and was determined to celebrate it without any disturbance.

The Passover meal was a celebration of the way in which God had brought the people of Israel out of their bondage in Egypt and set them on the road to the promised land. It was an occasion for reminding themselves of what God had done in establishing the nation and hence for praise and thanksgiving to him.

The continued offering of sacrifice year by year was an integral part of the feast, and its significance must not be overlooked. The Passover sacrifice was the only form of sacrifice in which the worshipper was personally involved in the slaying of the animal. The original Passover sacrifice at the time of the departure from Egypt was regarded as having redemptive significance. Although the yearly Passover sacrifice did not have all the characteristics of an offering made to atone for sin, nevertheless it was a sacrifice and thus a means of communion with God. At the same time it is probable that all sacrifices contained some element of atonement for sin, and it is unlikely that the Passover sacrifice was thought of any differently. Hence in Jewish thought the Passover sacrifice was one of the means through which God displayed his mercy to the people. We can say, therefore, that in broad terms the Passover sacrifice with its reminder of the original offering in Egypt had redemptive and expiatory associations and was seen as one of the ways in which the covenant between God and Israel was maintained in being.[2] When the Jews gathered together to celebrate the Passover meal with the lamb on the table, they were reminded of the covenant with their God in a very personal way.[3]

A further important factor in the celebration was its character as a family festival which emphasised that God's act of redemption is concerned not merely with individuals but with the creation of a people composed of families who will love and serve him.

Finally, the Passover had become an occasion for looking forward to the future redemption of Israel from its sorry plight at the coming of the Messiah. J. Jeremias has drawn attention to a prayer which is used at the Passover and other festivals, and which may go back to the first century; it contains a petition that God will remember the Messiah, the Son of David, in other words, that he will bring the Messiah to his people.[4] This is confirmed by a midrash on Psalm 118, which was one of the Psalms sung at the Passover, in which the coming of the Messiah is celebrated.[5] Indeed, there was a Jewish expectation that the Messiah would come during the night of the Passover. A Jewish poem describes the four nights on which God acted or will act for his people, and in each case it is the night of Nisan 15 which is meant. The four nights are the night of creation, the night of the covenant with Abraham, the night of the exodus from Egypt, and the night of future redemption:

> The Fourth Night, when the world shall have consummated its end to be delivered:
> The bands of iniquity will be destroyed and the bonds of iron will be broken;
> Moses will come forth from the desert, and King Messiah will come forth from Rome;
> The one will lead forth on the summit of a cloud and the other will lead forth on the summit of a cloud
> And the Memra of Jahweh will lead between them; and they shall go together.[6]

Although the dating of this poem and other Jewish material to the same effect is uncertain, it may well be that the ideas expressed go back to the first century and should be reckoned among the concepts associated with the celebration of the Passover.

If the meal which Jesus celebrated with his disciples was the Passover meal, or even if it was simply a meal held just before the Passover and therefore surrounded by paschal associations, it can be asserted that he held the meal because he wished to celebrate the Passover. This longing of Jesus to celebrate the Passover is conveyed in the words which come at the beginning of Luke's account of the meal: 'I have earnestly desired to eat this passover with you before I suffer' (Luke 22:15). Even if this saying is a composition by Luke based on Mark 14:25, it would still convey accurately enough the spirit in which Jesus came to the upper room. Jesus is a Jew who looks back to the act of redemption in which God had revealed his kingly, saving power for his people, and after which he had made his covenant with them in the wilderness of Sinai.

We may also presume that Jesus looked forward to the future act of redemption in which God would again act as he had done at the exodus from Egypt. As we have seen, the Jewish evidence for this hope must be evaluated with some caution. Nevertheless, the fact that Jesus himself shared this hope is evident from his own words at the meal. He spoke of eating the Passover again when 'it is fulfilled in the kingdom of God' (Luke 22:16). Similarly, we are told that Jesus took a cup of wine and spoke of drinking it again when 'the kingdom of God comes' (Luke 22:18), or, if we follow Mark's version, he spoke of the day when he would 'drink it new in the kingdom of God' (Mark 14:25). Whichever version of these words we regard as original, common to them all is the hope of a future celebration of the Passover in a new way. Thus there is a strong emphasis on the element of future expectation, or rather of certain hope, in the sayings of Jesus. Jesus, however, introduces a fresh element into the hope by speaking of the new Passover in the context of the kingdom of God. Moreover, it may be right to see in the words an allusion to the imminent fulfilment of this hope. Jesus' words may be taken to mean that there will not be another celebration of the Passover in the ordinary way before the era of fulfilment arrives.

But to what is Jesus referring? There may well be an allusion to the so-called messianic banquet, the meal which pious Jews expected to eat in heaven at the end of the age (Luke 14:15).[7] This meal can be associated with the resurrection of the pious men of old to share in it (Luke 13:28f.). But it has also been understood as the new meal which was to be celebrated in the church once the kingdom of God had come. In other words, the thought could be of the presence of Jesus with his disciples at the Lord's Supper. It is this idea that is surely present in the promise of the heavenly Lord to his people in Revelation 3:20: 'Behold, I stand at the door and knock; if any one hears my voice and opens the door, I will come in to him and eat with him and he with me'. While the promise contained here should not be confined to the Lord's presence in the Lord's Supper, it is surely right to include a reference to the Lord's Supper. Now it is certainly the case that the early church retained the hope of the future heavenly meal in the presence of Jesus (Rev. 19:9). We are, therefore, left in a dilemma as to whether the words of Jesus at the Last Supper should be taken as referring to the Lord's Supper or to the heavenly banquet.

The right solution may be the one offered by L. Goppelt who argues that Jesus' words indicated to the disciples that there would be an interval before they again sat at table with him; if so, what was going to happen in the meantime? Jesus answered this unspoken question by going on to describe how the disciples were to use bread and wine in the Lord's Supper.[8] If we adopt this solution we can say that Jesus looked forward to a new Passover in the heavenly kingdom of God, but that at the same time he commanded his disciples to celebrate a meal which would be an anticipation of that heavenly feast. We can thus regard the Lord's Supper as the feast of fulfilment in the kingdom of God inasmuch as it is an anticipation of the heavenly feast. Thus the Lord's Supper is linked to the Passover in that the Passover is a type of the heavenly banquet while the Lord's Supper is the anticipation of the heavenly banquet. The middle term of comparison between the Passover and the Lord's Supper is the heavenly banquet.[9]

If Jesus looked forward to the banquet in the kingdom of God in this way, two things would seem to follow. The first is that Jesus believed that God's act of redemption was near. The Last Supper was a Passover meal in which the accent shifted from remembering the past to anticipation of the future. It was, however, the past which set the pattern for the future. The events of the Exodus constituted the type which gave form to the future expectation of an act of redemption by the mighty hand of God. The second thing is that Jesus spoke in terms of fulfilment and newness, and thus indicated the end of the old Passover and its replacement by its fulfilment. Theologically the Passover came to an end with this final celebration by Jesus, and when the church would later speak of celebrating the festival (1 Cor. 5:7f.) it would be a new Christian festival that was regarded as paschal only insofar as the Passover provided the typology for understanding the death of Jesus as an act of redemption.

(2). *The farewell meal*

The words of Jesus which we have already been examining furnish a second insight into the nature of the Last Supper. It was a farewell meal. According to Luke Jesus wished to eat this meal before he suffered. The phrase 'before I suffer' stands under the suspicion of being Lucan in style, but the thought of Jesus' impending passion is implicit in the following verses when he says that he will not eat or drink again with his disciples, and it is strongly present in the prophecy of his betrayal. There is thus no good reason to doubt that the meal took place under the shadow of the departure of Jesus from his disciples.[10] By his unusual comments at the outset of the meal (if we follow Luke's

order of the sayings) Jesus forced his disciples to consideration
of what lay ahead both for himself and for them.

The force of this fact becomes all the stronger when we
recollect that the Last Supper was not an isolated event out of
the life of Jesus that we can separate off from the rest of the
story and consider on its own as if it had no connection with
what had preceded it. It is the merit of H. Patsch's important
study of the Last Supper and the historical Jesus that he has
attempted to place the meal firmly in its context in the ministry
of Jesus.[11] If we do this, we are faced (among other things) by
the fact that Jesus had become known to his disciples as the one
who had proclaimed in word and deed the coming of the kingdom
of God and in whom they had recognised the agent of God who
would bring in the kingdom. The words of the two travellers to
Emmaus aptly catch the mood of the disciples; they spoke about
'Jesus of Nazareth, who was a prophet mighty in deed and word
before God and all the people. ... We had hoped that he was the
one to redeem Israel' (Luke 24:19, 21). What had dashed their
hopes to the ground was that 'our chief priests and rulers
delivered him up to be condemned to death and crucified' (Luke
22:20). Something of this mood of shattered expectation must
already have been present as the shadows began to fall at the
Last Supper. With prophetic insight into what was shortly to
happen, Jesus was beginning to share his knowledge of his
departure with disciples who could scarcely understand what lay
ahead and could not bring it into harmony with their existing
hopes and ideas.

Jeremias has seen something further in Jesus' words, and this
is the appropriate point to comment on his interpretation.[12] He
takes Jesus to mean that he would not be partaking in the
Passover meal. 'I have earnestly desired to eat this passover with
you' is taken as the expression of a desire that was not fulfilled.
We can set aside the view that Jesus was speaking at a meal
shortly before the Passover and expressing his unfulfillable
desire to eat the actual Passover meal that would not take place
until he had died.[13] Jeremias takes the words to mean that Jesus
abstained from the food placed on the table in front of him and
that likewise he did not drink the wine which he offered to his
disciples. The words are not simply the expression of an unfulfilled wish but represent rather a declaration of intent or an
oath by which Jesus resolved not to take part in the meal.
Jeremias finds this interpretation confirmed by two things. First,
he holds that it is unlikely that Jesus would have partaken of

food which he was to use as a symbol of his own body and blood. Second, he refers to the practice of the Quartodecimans[14] who used to fast during the Jewish Passover night until cockcrow when they celebrated the Lord's Supper; Jeremias argues that this early Christian practice must have been modelled on the example of Jesus himself. The question then arises as to why Jesus abstained from the meal, and Jeremias's answer is that he was fasting and thereby praying and interceding for the people of Israel. In this way he set an example which was followed by the early church which fasted for its persecutors and especially for the Jews.

This interpretation has been analysed carefully by Patsch. He points out that the linguistic basis for the view that Jesus was deliberately abstaining from the meal is uncertain; the texts can be understood equally well to mean that Jesus did take part in the meal. The argument that Jesus himself would not have partaken of a meal representing his own body and blood springs from later dogmatic theology. The practice of later Christians and their theological reasons for their practice cannot necessarily be traced back to Jesus. Moreover, if there really was a motif of intercession for the Jews in the passage, one would have expected some clearer evidence for it. Jesus' sayings in fact are concerned more with the coming of the kingdom than with intercession for the Jews. Although, therefore, this interpretation of the passage cannot be excluded as impossible (especially for Luke 22:18), it is not persuasive and reads a good deal into the text. Jesus was speaking about 'not eating again', not about 'fasting'.[15] This verdict would appear to be sound. The sayings on which Jeremias bases his interpretation are primarily statements about the future fulfilment of the Passover in the kingdom of God.

Jesus thus attempted to prepare his disciples for his departure from them. The close links between him and them on a physical plane were about to be broken. This was the last meal that he would share *with them*. This element of sharing together must not be underemphasised. The Last Supper was a fellowship meal between Jesus and his disciples, the culmination of the long period during which they had been joined together in a close relationship. The severance of that fellowship was all the more significant in the view of its deep character. This becomes especially apparent in John's description of the meal and the ensuing conversations between Jesus and the disciples.

(3). *The actions of Jesus*

H. Schürmann has been especially responsible for drawing attention to the possible significance of the actions of Jesus at the Last Supper. He is prepared to admit that we cannot attain to any certainty about what Jesus actually said at the meal. Even when we have worked back to the earliest recoverable form of the tradition, we still cannot be historically sure that we possess the *ipsissima verba* of Jesus. Consequently, it is all the more significant that the various accounts of the meal in the different traditions agree in describing what Jesus did at the meal. We can discover the *ipsissima facta* of Jesus, and these can throw an important light on the meaning of the meal.[16]

The facts basically correspond with Jewish practice at a meal. The host took bread, gave thanks on behalf of the guests, then broke off a piece for each person and gave it to them. At the end of the meal he took a cup of wine in his hand, gave thanks on behalf of the guests, and then drank from it. According to Schürmann, each guest then drank from his own cup, although we have already seen that there is some doubt about this and that it is possible that a common cup was the usual practice.[17]

So far there is nothing unusual about these actions. What is unusual is the way in which the actions are described in such a detailed manner if they were perfectly normal. In describing a modern meal one would not go into details about how the table was set and the food prepared and served unless what was happening was unusual in some way or significant for the story as a whole. Thus, if somebody was poisoned as a result of eating a meal, a knowledge of how the food was prepared could be very important in discovering the course of events that led to the tragedy. It can, therefore, be assumed that the detailed description of the procedure at the Last Supper was significant. Even if the description was meant primarily as a pattern to be followed at the Lord's Supper, it was still important to follow out this particular pattern. Schürmann comments on the fact that the early church took the two actions of Jesus with the bread and the cup and singled them out as the important features of the Lord's Supper; he argues that it is significant that the church placed together two actions which originally were separated by the length of the meal.

There were, however, according to Schürmann, two features which made the actions of Jesus unusual. The first of these is that, contrary to custom, Jesus shared his own cup of wine with the disciples instead of letting them drink from their own cups.

According to Schürmann this action gave the disciples a share
in the blessing attached to the cup, just as the distribution of
the bread gave them a share in the blessing attached to it. There
are unfortunately two dubious points about this exposition.
First, we have just seen that it is not certain that Jesus was
acting contrary to custom in sharing his cup with the disciples.
However, the way in which the accounts emphasise that all the
disciples drank from the cup may well suggest that the early
church saw significance in what Jesus did and tip the balance in
favour of Schürmann's interpretation. The second uncertain
point is that, as we noted earlier, the idea of blessing being
conveyed by sharing in the bread and wine seems very dubious.[18]
Schürmann rejects G. Dalman's view which is surely more probable, namely that by sharing in the bread and wine the guests
shared in the thanksgiving to God which had been spoken on
their behalf, and to that extent they were doing an action which
was pleasing to God and made them the objects of his favour.[19]
The significance of the offering of the bread and wine to the
disciples must therefore be sought elsewhere.

This point brings us to the second unusual feature in the
conduct of Jesus. This is the simple fact that, whatever may
have been his actual words, Jesus did accompany the distribution
of the bread and wine with some interpretative sayings. He said
something to explain why he was giving the bread and wine to
the disciples. This feature can certainly be taken as historical
fact. Moreover, it appears to be genuinely unusual in that no
Jewish parallels have been brought forward to explain it. The
nearest parallel is the Passover *haggadah* in which the symbolic significance of the various features of the meal was
explained, but the Passover explanations did not accompany the
distribution of the food in the same way as here. We have thus
a feature which is intelligible in a Palestinian milieu but which
is not paralleled in it, and hence we can invoke here the criterion
of dissimilarity in confirmation of the historicity of the
account.[20]

What, then, is the significance of these actions? Although we
have denied that the idea of participating in the blessing
associated with the bread and wine is present, it remains true
that the food is presented to the disciples as a gift and that food
is particularly suited to be a symbol of salvation. Hence the
distribution of the bread and wine can be seen, first, as a symbol
of a gift to the disciples.

It is important that the bread and wine are actually received by the disciples. The action indicates not merely the offering of a gift but the reception of a gift. By accepting what Jesus gave to them the disciples accepted the symbolical significance of the gift and thus gave their assent to his offer. Thus in due course the Lord's Supper became a sign not simply of the offer of salvation but also of the reception of salvation.[21]

A second factor is that the meal may be seen as symbolical of the future messianic banquet in the kingdom of God, especially since Jesus himself had earlier spoken in his ministry of this banquet and of its relation to the kingdom of God. A third factor is that in the context of the impending departure of Jesus he may have been giving his disciples a prophetic symbol of the significance of his death. However, this interpretation of the actions of Jesus is assured only when they are seen in the light of the actual words of interpretation. For the moment the most that can be said is that the significance given to the actions by the words of interpretation is entirely congruous with the nature of the actions themselves.

(4). *The significance of the bread*

From the actions performed by Jesus which demanded some kind of interpretation we turn now to the interpretation itself. Although the narrative brings together the distribution of the bread and the wine so that the two sayings of Jesus illuminate each other, we must remember that at the Last Supper the two actions and the corresponding sayings were separated by the meal, so that it is right to examine them separately. We therefore look at the significance of the bread first of all. The distribution was introduced by the normal procedure at a Jewish meal, and the giving of thanks was for the bread as food and as a sign of God's goodness. The novel feature lay in the comment of Jesus, 'This is my body which is given for you. Do this in remembrance of me'. If we follow the Marcan form of the saying, Jesus prefaced the statement about his body with the word 'Take', which confirms the interpretation of his action as the offer of a gift to the disciples. The significance of the gift is then that it is said to be the body of Jesus.

The word 'is', which would have been absent from an original saying in Hebrew or Aramaic, can mean 'signify' as well as 'be identical with', and there can be no doubt whatever that at the Last Supper the word was used with the former meaning. The saying was uttered by Jesus while he was bodily present with the disciples, and they could see that his body and the bread were two separate things.[22] One might compare how a person showing a photograph of himself to a group of friends could say, as he points to it, 'This is me'. In any case, Jesus had done nothing to the bread which could have changed its character; all that he had done was to give thanks to God for it, not to bless or consecrate it in any way.

There is an unresolved argument concerning the precise meaning of the word *sōma*, translated 'body'. G. Dalman argued that it was equivalent to an Aramaic word *gûpā* which means the person as a whole ('body' in contrast to 'soul').[23] J. Jeremias, however, has advocated the view that the corresponding Aramaic word is *bi'srā* which means 'flesh' as opposed to 'bones' or 'blood'. If we adopt this view, then the reference could be to the two parts of the body which are separated in a sacrifice, the flesh and the blood.[24] In this connection it is sometimes suggested that the breaking of the bread symbolises the breaking of the body of Jesus in death. But this is improbable. 'Breaking' is not an appropriate metaphor for killing, and the breaking of the bread is simply the preliminary to its distribution.[25] The view that Jesus was referring to his flesh has, however, been strongly contested. It is argued that the parallelism of 'body' and 'blood' is found only in the Marcan form of the sayings and not in the possibly earlier Lucan/Pauline form; that the two sayings were originally separated by the meal and each saying was meant to be complete in itself; and that the rendering of *bi'srā* by *sōma* rather than by *sarx* is improbable.[26] However, even if we accept Dalman's view, a sacrificial sense is still required, since Jesus would then be speaking of giving himself or his person as a whole. E. Schweizer, who adopts this view, says that 'body' represents the 'I' in its totality, while 'blood' represents the 'I' in the act of dying. A decision between the two views is not easy. Once the bread-saying and the cup-saying were placed in parallel, as in Mark, the tendency would certainly be to think in terms of the flesh and blood of Jesus given in sacrifice, and we can see this tendency reflected in the use of 'flesh' and 'blood' in John 6:51. However, the linguistic evidence, especially as presented by H. Patsch, speaks against the likelihood of *sōma* being a translation of *bi'srā*, and thus it seems more probable that the flesh/blood contrast is a later development.

We can take it, then, that Jesus used the bread to represent himself. But in what sense did he mean this? One possibility is that he was speaking of himself as the source of spiritual nourishment for his disciples. R. Pesch suggests that he was interpreting himself as the source of blessing and salvation and thus offering a share in fellowship with him as the Messiah to the disciples.[27] This interpretation is possible only with the Marcan form of the saying which contains no further elucidation of the term 'body'. Pesch is admittedly prepared to go further and say that an interpretation of his death can be found in this saying, an interpretation which is set off against his messiahship.[28] However, he does not develop this idea in any way.

This thought of spiritual nourishment is found in John 6, and it is a correct understanding of the total intention of Jesus. Nevertheless, it is very doubtful whether it does justice to the saying. In the first place, it goes well beyond the simple phrase 'This is my body' and seems to read into it more than is justifiable without some further indication that this was the meaning intended by Jesus. To suggest that it is confirmed by the Marcan context with its presentation of Jesus as Messiah and Son of man is not convincing, since the idea of communion with the Messiah as a means of salvation is not present. In the second place, the saying was seen by the Marcan tradition in the light of the cup-saying. Even though the two sayings were originally separate, we must surely grant that Jesus intended the two sayings to be in some way complementary to each other. If, then, the second saying speaks of Jesus' sacrificial death, we should expect something similar to be present in the former saying. In the third place, the saying in its Marcan form is enigmatic. The interpretation which we are considering lacks a firm basis in the brief text. But there is an elucidation in the Lucan/Pauline form of the text, and we have already seen that there are strong arguments for regarding this as the original form of the saying. Even if this is not the case, the Lucan/Pauline form at least represents an early exegesis of the saying and demands respect on that account.

If we take this longer form of the saying into account, the phrase 'which is given for you' makes good sense as a prophetic utterance about the imminent death of Jesus.[29] The phraseology reflects Old Testament and Jewish language, and can be used of making a sacrifice[30] or of the self-giving of a martyr on behalf of others.[31] Attempts to make the meaning of the saying more precise are as follows: (a). If we move beyond saying that Jesus speaks of himself in general sacrificial terms, the question inevitably arises in the context of the Passover as to whether Jesus thought of himself as the Passover sacrifice. According to J. Jeremias, 'he is *the eschatological paschal lamb*, representing the

fulfilment of all that of which the Egyptian paschal lamb and all
the subsequent sacrificial paschal lambs were the prototype'.[32]
This interpretation clearly goes beyond anything in the saying
itself and must be derived from the context. Jeremias holds that
in the Passover *haggadah* Jesus had already interpreted the lamb
as referring to himself. Such an interpretation has to face some
obstacles. First, we must recognise that there is some uncertainty
whether the Passover meal of Jesus was celebrated with a lamb.
The synoptic Gospels certainly assume that a lamb was used,[33]
but some scholars doubt whether a lamb would have been available for a meal in advance of the proper official time. Second,
there is no record in the accounts of the meal that Jesus compared himself to the lamb. It is arguable that such a significant
piece of symbolism would not have been left unmentioned.
Third, if it is maintained that the comparison of Jesus to the
Passover lamb is well attested in the NT, it can be replied that
this comparison could very well have been developed on the basis
of Jesus' death at the Passover season, and possibly even at the
actual time when the Passover lambs were being sacrificed.
Fourth, if the Lord's Supper was celebrated more frequently
than once a year, it can be urged that it would be natural to
drop those elements in the narrative of the Last Supper which
could not be reproduced at the Lord's Supper. The case as a
whole is hardly a strong one, and we cannot say with certainty
that Jesus compared himself specifically to the Passover lamb.
At most we can say that the Passover setting of the meal and the
way in which it looks forward to a new Passover in the kingdom
of God must have raised the question of a replacement for the
Passover sacrifice.

(b). A second possibility is that Jesus saw his approaching
death in terms of the sacrifice which inaugurates a covenant
between God and man. This understanding is clearly present in
the cup-saying, and we shall return to it later, but there is
nothing in the bread-saying by itself to suggest this particular
interpretation.

(c). A third possibility is that Jesus was comparing his death
to that of a martyr who dies for the people as a whole. The use
of sacrificial language in this way is found especially in 4
Maccabees. When Eleazar was being tortured to death, he said,
'Thou, O God, knowest that though I might save myself I am
dying by fiery torments for thy Law. Be merciful unto thy
people, and let our punishment be a satisfaction in their behalf.
Make my blood their purification, and take my soul to ransom

their souls.' (4 Macc. 6:28f.). Later the writer comments on the deaths of the martyrs: 'Through them the enemy had no more power over our people, and the tyrant suffered punishment, and our country was purified, they having as it were become a ransom for our nation's sin; and through the blood of these righteous men and the propitiation of their death, the divine Providence delivered Israel that before was evil entreated' (4 Macc. 17:21f.). There can be no doubt that Jesus expected a martyr's death, and it is very probable that he saw his death in this general manner.[34]

(d). Although the literature of Jewish martyrdom makes no reference to the fate of the suffering Servant of Yahweh described in Isaiah 52:13–53:12, the Servant is the supreme example of martyrdom, and it is certain that Jesus had this figure in mind when he referred to his own impending death. The idea of giving himself reflects Is. 53:10. The phrase 'for you' is to be understood as equivalent to the phrase 'for many' in the cup-saying in Mark. We have already argued that here the Marcan form is original, even if the phrase has been shifted from its original position in the bread-word. 'For many/you' is a clear echo of Is. 53:11f.; none of the alternative explanations of the phrase is as probable as this one.[35] Jesus thus envisaged himself as the Servant who carries the sin of the people, pours himself out in death, and so achieves reconciliation with God. The language used in Is. 53 to describe the work of the Servant is sacrificial, and Jesus takes this concept over to explain his own death.

The differing interpretations of the sacrificial significance of the death of Jesus which we have surveyed are in no way competitors with one another. It is possible to combine them and to argue that Jesus saw himself as fulfilling several different Old Testament types simultaneously. This would be entirely consistent with what we know from elsewhere in the Gospels of his self-understanding as the One who fulfils the Law and the Prophets.

Finally, as the last part of the saying over the bread we have the command of Jesus that the disciples should 'do this' in remembrance of him. 'Do this' must refer to the action of Jesus in breaking and sharing the bread which he wished his disciples to continue to do during his absence. The most obvious explanation of these words is that Jesus wished his disciples to carry out this action in order that they might remember him, and more specifically so that they might remember the significance of his death for them. Such an interpretation would fit in very well

with the emphasis of the Passover meal at which the People of
Israel called to mind what God had done for them at the Exodus
and identified themselves as the recipients of the divine redemption (Ex. 12:14; 13:9). There is no need to link the thought of
remembrance with Hellenistic cult meals in which the dead were
commemorated. Quite apart from the fact that there is an
adequate background in Jewish thinking, there is the simple fact
that for the disciples of Jesus he was not a dead hero of the past
but the living Lord. In any case, this kind of interpretation presupposes that the saying is not authentic, whereas we have
argued that it may well go back to Jesus himself.

However, a different interpretation of the saying against its
Jewish background has been proposed by J. Jeremias who thinks
that it is a request to carry out the Lord's Supper in order that
God may remember Jesus and specifically that he may do so by
causing the kingdom to come at the parousia. Jeremias argues
that when Paul says 'you proclaim the Lord's death until he
comes' there is really an element of purpose in the last clause,
so that it means 'you proclaim the Lord's death until the goal
is reached that he comes' and he links this hope with the early
church prayer 'Maranatha'. He bases the substance of his case on
Jewish material in which various actions are done for a memorial
to God, *i.e.* in order that he may be reminded to act in a certain
way.[36] This view is not very probable. So far as Paul's statement
is concerned, while it is probable that the clause 'until he comes'
contains an element of purpose,[37] the proclamation which is
described is a proclamation of the gospel to men and there is no
suggestion that it is a proclamation to God. As for the Jewish
material, it has been shown that when the phraseology is used in
the Old Testament a reference to divine remembering is always
indicated by the actual mention of God in the context.[38] The
basis for Jeremias's view is thus rendered doubtful, and it remains more likely that the remembering of his death is done by
the disciples. The action is to remind them of Jesus.

Indeed, this is surely what is required by the context. For the
problem at issue is how the disciples may continue to remain
attached to Jesus during his physical absence. The answer to the
problem is that by celebrating the Lord's Supper they remember
him, and they remember him in the same kind of way as the
Jews remembered the Passover and thought of themselves as
partakers in the act of redemption. The God who had brought
Israel out of Egypt continued to be their God, and similarly the
relationship which Jesus had with his disciples during his

ministry continues to be real after his death. The proclamation of the gospel in the breaking of bread and the sharing of the cup makes the saving event real for all generations.[39]

(5). *The significance of the cup*

After the main course of the meal Jesus and his disciples shared the so-called 'cup of blessing', and again he proceeded to interpret the significance of his action. If we consider first the wording which is common to Luke and to Mark, Jesus refers to his blood 'which is shed for you/many'. As we have seen, this phrase may be a secondary parallel to the similar phrase in the bread-saying. Its significance is in any case the same and requires no further elucidation. Jesus is thinking of his death as that of the suffering Servant on behalf of mankind. The important new element is the comparison of the cup and its contents to his blood. The term blood has undoubtedly the thoughts of death and sacrifice attached to it. It is impossible to rid the saying of the thought of the death of Jesus, since there is no other meaning that blood can convey here; it spoke of death, and especially of violent death. The thought of a sacrificial death is hardly less escapable. It was the blood of the sacrificial animal which made atonement in the Old Testament sacrificial system. Here one specific type of sacrifice is in mind. It is 'the new covenant in my blood' or, as Mark has it, 'my blood of the covenant'.

A number of scholars have claimed that this idea cannot go back to Jesus since the Marcan form of the wording cannot be turned back into Aramaic. The argument has always been a dubious one since it may mean little more than 'we modern scholars do not know how to translate this back into Aramaic'. It can be set aside all the more confidently since it is now recognised that there is no real difficulty about providing an acceptable paraphrase of the words.[40] In any case, the Marcan form of the wording may be secondary to the form in Luke and Paul.[41] Since all our sources contain the covenant idea and since there is no good reason for denying that Jesus could have used it, we are justified in regarding it as an integral part of the saying.

Two Old Testament passages lie at the root of the concept as used here. The first is Exodus 24:8 where we learn how the covenant in the wilderness was instituted with a sacrifice. Moses made an offering to God, took the blood of the animal, and sprinkled it upon the people with the words, 'Behold the blood of the covenant which the Lord has made with you'. The second passage is Jeremiah 31:31–34, which refers to the new covenant which God was going to make with the people of Israel and Judah. The latter passage says nothing about blood, and hence if the Lucan/Pauline form of words is original with its explicit allusion to Jeremiah there must also be an implicit reference to Exodus as well. On the other hand, if the Marcan form is original, with its clear reference to Exodus and its omission of the key word 'new', it is arguable that the allusion to Jeremiah is a secondary development in the saying. However, if this is the case, and we owe the clear reference to Jeremiah to some early Christian rather than to the actual words of Jesus, the fact remains that in talking of a covenant sealed with his own blood Jesus was undoubtedly talking of *another* covenant, different from the one made in the wilderness and hence a new covenant. That the word 'new' was in the mind of Jesus is seen from Mark 1, if that gives us the original wording of this saying. It is an open question whether the use of the word there demonstrates that the thought of newness was present in the mind of Jesus or provided the key word for an early Christian to bring out the intended meaning of Jesus' saying about the convenant more clearly.

The sacrifice which inaugurated the covenant in the wilderness was intended to atone for the sins of the people so that they might then belong to God in a covenant relationship. This point has been emphasised by R. Pesch who has drawn attention to the way in which the Targum on Exodus 24:7f. stresses the atoning effect of the blood which was thrown against the altar by Moses.[42] The sacrifice was in effect the means authorised by God for cleansing the people from their sins. By analogy, therefore, Jesus here interprets his own death as a substitutionary sacrifice for the sins of the people that they may become partakers in the new covenant. Hence the concepts of the covenant and of the suffering Servant who bears the sins of the many fit in with one another and form a unified whole (*cf.* Is. 42:6; 49:8). There is a fundamental unity between them which means that they belong together theologically and neither of them need be regarded as a secondary development of an originally simpler interpretation of the death of Jesus.

Finally, there is the idea of the covenant itself. We have learned in recent years to recognise more clearly that a covenant is a relationship, usually a one-sided one in which a superior party imposes his will on an inferior and bestows various advantages on him, in return for which he expects the inferior to fulfil various stipulations. Such a relationship is initiated by a solemn ceremony which binds the partners to each other. This type of relationship has been studied in various vassal-treaties from Old Testament times, and it has been seen that the covenant relationship between Yahweh and the people of Israel was expressed in language which is familiar in ancient diplomacy.[43] Yahweh made promises to the Israelites and claimed them as his people, laying down the various obligations which they were to observe towards him. This relationship is of fundamental importance in the thought of the Old Testament. When the covenant relationship was damaged by the failure of Israel to keep its obligations, Yahweh promised through Jeremiah that he would make a new covenant with the people in which he would write his laws on their hearts rather than on tablets of stone and in which the sins of the people would be forgiven and they would all know, *i.e.* love and serve, God. It can be debated how far this concept was completely 'new'; the ideals expressed by Jeremiah could be said to have been an intended part of the first covenant with Moses.[44] There is no doubt, however, that the New Testament writers saw the fulfilment of Jeremiah's prophecy in the new covenant which Jesus claimed to establish by his sacrificial death. Here in his saying at the Last Supper we have the basis for their conviction that they lived in the era of the new covenant. The death of Jesus represents God's sovereign disposition of grace to the people.

From these comments we can now see how rich is the complex of ideas which is contained in the actions and sayings of Jesus at the Last Supper. The whole of the brief narrative is charged with meaning and offers us deep insights into the mind of Jesus as he approached his death.

THE LAST SUPPER IN THE GOSPEL OF MARK

Before we can regard our study of the Last Supper as complete two tasks remain to be undertaken. On the one hand, we must ask ourselves how the account which we have just been studying fits into the historical life of Jesus. Can we say that the Last Supper fits appropriately into the ministry of Jesus, and are there any features in his ministry which may shed further light upon it? On the other hand, we must also trace the way in which the Evangelists have incorporated the account into their Gospels since this too may shed light on the event and show what the early church made of it. Since our information about the historical Jesus comes from the Gospels, these two enquiries are closely connected. Rather than pursue them separately, we shall find it most convenient to take them together, especially since in our opinion there is good reason to accept the general historical reliability of the Gospels as accounts of the ministry of Jesus.[45] We shall direct our attention to each of the synoptic Gospels in turn, beginning with Mark.

We have already touched on some of the historical problems which surround the teaching of Jesus at the Last Supper. Thus we have already referred briefly to the question whether Jesus expected to die a violent death; without entering into a detailed discussion of the point we have noted that there is good reason to believe that he accepted this possibility.[46] Again, we have asked whether Jesus expected the end of the world to come so quickly that there would be no point in his appointing a rite for his followers to observe regularly during his absence from them, and we have claimed that Jesus anticipated an interval of uncertain extent before the consummation.[47] Both of these points form part of a question which can be expressed more theologically. The message of Jesus was concerned with the rule of God and the effects which it would bring for mankind in judgment and salvation. If Jesus proclaimed the rule of God, how can the thought of his own death be brought into harmony with that expectation? What room was there in his message for the thought of his death as a means of bringing blessing to men? Can the idea of sacrifice find a place in the theology of the kingdom of God?

A full answer to questions such as these would almost demand a study of the entire ministry and teaching of Jesus, but we must content ourselves with some limited observations which, it is hoped, will be sufficient to show the general lines of a solution to the problem. Two main points require discussion.

(1). *The fellowship of the kingdom*

In Mark, as in the other Gospels, Jesus' message of the kingdom is presented as good news. It is the announcement that the time has arrived for the fulfilment of prophecy and that God's rule is at hand. We can leave the question open whether Mark 1:15 refers to the presence of the kingdom or its imminence, although our own preference is for the former interpretation. In either case the message and ministry of Jesus brought to people an immediate experience of the saving power of God. Jesus certainly announced that the End was near and urged people to be ready for it, but at the same time he also brought the blessings of God's rule to them as present realities. He proclaimed both the imminent futurity and the presence of the rule of God, a combination that is in no way strange since the rule of God was for him an expression that meant 'God acting in saving power' regardless of time. It is one of the decisive advances in recent scholarship that the sterile either/or of futurist *versus* realised eschatology has been replaced by a recognition that Jesus saw God's rule as active both in the present and in the future.[48] This means that we can do full justice to the character of Jesus' ministry as the era of fulfilment in which the blessings of salvation became real and actual for those who were willing to receive them.[49] During the ministry of Jesus the hoped-for future blessings of God's rule could be experienced as present realities, even if they were experienced partially in a world which was still part of the old age.

Among these blessings must be numbered the way in which Jesus welcomed and forgave those who were regarded as outcasts from the religious society of his day and were branded as 'tax collectors and sinners'. One particular form in which this welcome was expressed was in the table-fellowship which Jesus extended to such people. This fellowship was both a sign of forgiveness and acceptance and also an anticipation of the heavenly meal when all God's people are gathered round his table.[50] The Gospels attach considerable significance to the meals celebrated by Jesus, and we are right to claim that they were not just occasions for satisfying hunger or for human friendship and festivity but were fraught with theological significance. In the last analysis to eat with Jesus was to share in fellowship with the Messiah as God's Agent who brings his blessings to men and thus to anticipate the heavenly feast at the table of God.

It makes good sense to see the Last Supper against this background, as part of the series of meals which Jesus had with his disciples and to which he invited the poor and needy. The Last Supper brings to focus the ideas which are less distinctly present in the earlier meals of Jesus. It is an occasion for fellowship with Jesus and a pledge of a future fellowship with him in a new way through the bread and the cup.

It is inevitable that in this context our attention is directed particularly to two passages in Mark which describe how Jesus fed a large number of people with a meagre quantity of food, consisting of the bread and fish which would have been the normal kind of fare for people having a packed meal in the open-

air. The significance of these two stories is complex, but one
element that cannot be overlooked is the way in which the action
of Jesus is described: he took the loaves, said the blessing, broke
the loaves and gave them to the disciples (Mark 6:41; *cf.* 8:6).
This formulation is reminiscent of the phraseology used to
describe the action of Jesus at the Last Supper. The resemblances
are not surprising, since the gestures were the normal action of
the host at a Jewish meal and on each occasion Jesus was
involved in distributing food to guests. One might be tempted
to conclude, therefore, that nothing more is being described than
the usual procedure at a meal. But this explanation is hardly
adequate. For, first, it is hard to see why the Evangelists
recorded a normal procedure at such length; the view that they
were merely showing how the normal action of Jesus led to a
miraculous result is not a sufficient explanation. Second, there
are clear signs in the narratives of an increasing assimilation of
the wording to that of the Last Supper narratives.[51] It is thus
probable that from at least an early stage in the tradition some
relationship between the feeding miracles and the Last Supper
was recognised. Congregations who heard the stories of the
miracles were in effect being directed to the relationship between
the miracles and the Last Supper.

However, it is one thing to see resemblances in the stories and
another to see them in the mind of Jesus. Some commentators
have gone so far as to speak of a Galilean 'Lord's Supper', but
this is an exaggeration. There is no Passover setting in the
synoptic Gospels (but see John 6:4), and the persons fed were
not necessarily disciples. Here the disciples function as Jesus'
helpers in feeding the crowd. In no sense can fish be equated
with wine, and above all there are no interpretative sayings by
Jesus. There is no connection between the stories and the death
of Jesus. It is clear that the Last Supper is in no sense anticipated in the feeding miracles, except in that both were occasions
of fellowship with Jesus and both involved the satisfaction of
hunger by Jesus. Just as Jesus used bread and wine at the Last
Supper as symbols of spiritual food and drink, so the early
church saw in the feeding miracles the symbolic representation
of Jesus' provision of spiritual nourishment. If we are entitled
to see in the feeding miracles an antitype to the provision of the
manna and a foreshadowing of the heavenly banquet, then it is
justifiable to regard the stories as symbolical of spiritual
nourishment and so as testimonies to the same spiritual truth as
is expressed in the Last Supper. But while the early church

recognised these motifs in the stories of miraculous feeding, we cannot be sure how far they go back to the mind of Jesus himself.[52]

We can, then, see the Last Supper as an example of the table-fellowship through which Jesus bound his disciples closely to him and as a foretaste of the heavenly banquet; the feeding miracle stories fall within this general framework, but, although the early church regarded them as in some sense anticipations of the Last Supper, there is no real justification for regarding them as 'eucharistic' in the proper sense of the term.

(2). *The opposition to Jesus*

Right from the beginning of his Gospel Mark includes stories which show that the message of Jesus roused opposition especially from the religious people of his day. Jesus cut across the mass of human regulations which were in danger of obscuring the real intent of the revelation of God in the Old Testament, and he attacked the kind of religion that went only skindeep, that presented a facade of piety beneath which lay pride and greed. But of particular importance in the present context is the way in which the attitude of Jesus to sinful people earned him the scorn and opposition of the Pharisees. 'Why does he eat with tax collectors and sinners?' (Mark 2:16) was their indignant question. They went so far as to attribute his exorcisms and other mighty works to the power of Beelzebub or Satan. In short, it was the message of the saving rule of God which brought Jesus into disfavour with the Jewish authorities, and they rejected the possibility that he was God's Agent. This meant that Jesus' mission was far from being universally successful. On the contrary, from a human point of view it seemed to be destined for failure. The task of Jesus could not be accomplished by the means which he used. There was no question of a national renewal of Judaism as a result of his ministry.

Behind this rejection of himself and his message Jesus evidently saw the same kind of blindness of heart and stiffnecked opposition to God and his messengers which had characterised the Jews down the ages. It is not surprising that he realised that his mission could lead him to martyrdom. And against the background of the Jewish understanding of the significance of martyrdom it would again not be surprising if he saw his own death in the same kind of way. The opposition to him sprang from human sin and rejection of God.

It follows from all this that Jesus saw his contemporaries as standing under divine judgment and warned them of it. He foresaw the sad fate of Jerusalem which rejected the prophets. He spoke of the danger of men being rejected by the Son of man at the End because they had not responded to the call to discipleship. And in a significant saying he took up the thought of Psalm 49:7f. with its declaration that no man can ransom himself from the power of the grave. 'What can a man give in return for his life?' (Mark 8:37). The implied answer is 'Nothing'.

It is against this background that we can appreciate an important saying recorded by Mark. In an important passage (Mark 10:35–45) Jesus spoke of the necessity of serving others; true greatness lies in willingness to serve. This was the attitude that characterised his own life; the cliché which describes Jesus as 'the Man for others' has been overworked, but it contains the heart of the gospel. It is against the backdrop of the opposition to him that we can see the essential character of the One who proclaimed the rule of God as the One who cared for the needy no matter what the cost. This attitude is expressed in the saying that 'the Son of man also came not to be served but to serve, and to give his life as a ransom for many' (Mark 10:45). Here in this saying we find that the death of Jesus, which might be interpreted merely as the crowning example of his life of self-sacrifice and self-giving love for others, or as the culmination of a campaign of opposition to him, is in fact regarded as somehow conveying a blessing to mankind. The language which is used here is similar to that used of the martyrs in the Maccabean literature; more important, it echoes the thought of Isaiah 53 and contains the clear sacrificial notion of death on behalf of others. If man cannot ransom his life, the point is surely that here is One who can ransom man; the Psalmist's hope, 'But God will ransom my soul from the power of Sheol' (Psalm 49:15), here finds its fulfilment.[53]

The passage clearly prepares the way for the sayings of Jesus at the Last Supper. In other words, the Last Supper is not a foreign body within the Gospel of Mark but fits naturally into a sequence of presentation of the ministry of Jesus which emphasises both the fact of opposition to Jesus leading to his martyrdom and the fact that Jesus foresaw his death and understood it creatively as a means of ransoming mankind through substitutionary sacrifice. The atmosphere of opposition and evil plotting surrounds the Last Supper and is expressed most poignantly in the prophecy of the betrayal of Jesus by one of the Twelve. The recognition by Jesus that his 'way' must lead to a death with a redemptive function comes to fulness of expression at the Supper.

Whether Mark's presentation corresponds with the historical facts has of course been much debated. We have already indicated that Jesus doubtless anticipated his violent death. Whether he saw that death as having a special significance is more controversial. A verdict depends on our estimate of the 'Son of man' sayings which speak of the divinely-based necessity of his death (Mark 8:31; 9:12, 31; 10:33f.) and especially of the ransom saying (Mark 10:45). Although these sayings continue to be regarded as inauthentic by various scholars, I would claim that at the very least they contain authentic elements of the teaching of Jesus in which he anticipated his own suffering and vindication.[54] The case for the authenticity of Mark 10:45 has been stated by J. Jeremias, and subsequent attacks on the saying have not in my opinion overthrown his case.[55]

We would thus claim that the Last Supper of Jesus is of a piece with his earlier ministry and can be understood as fitting in harmoniously with his earlier teaching about the rule of God and his own place in relation to its establishment. Mark's account of the ministry of Jesus is a faithful reflection of the historical facts.

THE LAST SUPPER IN THE GOSPEL OF MATTHEW

We do not need to spend time looking at the account of the Last Supper in the total context of the Gospel of Matthew. Matthew's account of the ministry of Jesus is not essentially different from that of Mark, and there is no indication that he understood Jesus' message of the kingdom and his own relationship to the kingdom in a significantly different manner. All that we need to do, therefore, is to take a look at the Last Supper narrative itself and note whether there are any significant changes in it from the Marcan presentation.

Like Mark, Matthew has the prophecy by Jesus that somebody will betray him before the eucharistic account. But while Mark does not record who the betrayer was to be – a fact already known to the readers from a previous section (Mark 14:10f.), Matthew tells us that Judas asked, 'Is it I, Master?' and Jesus replied, 'You have said so,' a form of words which leaves the decision to betray Jesus and the responsibility of doing so firmly in the lap of Judas.[56] If anything, the conversation stresses the enormity of the betrayal, and thus heightens the way in which the eucharistic account is framed by prophecies of betrayal and desertion. The contrast between the weakness and sinfulness of the disciples and the action of Jesus in offering them the signs of salvation which we find in Mark is thus continued in Matthew.

In the actual account of the meal, Jesus' saying over the bread contains a specific command to eat it, which fills out the meaning of Mark's 'Take'. In the same way the command 'Drink of it, all of you' appears in the cup-saying and replaces the Marcan narrative statement 'and they all drank of it'. These two alterations are probably best regarded as stemming from liturgical practice, but at the same time the effect is that Matthew, like Luke and Paul, describes exclusively what Jesus did and makes no mention of what the disciples did.[57]

The most significant alteration, however, is that Matthew adds the phrase 'for the forgiveness of sins' to the cup-saying to describe the purpose of the shedding of Jesus' blood. This is a fresh theological concept. Since there is already a reference to the covenant in the cup-saying, which alludes to the new covenant in Jeremiah 31:31–34, it is likely that the reference to the forgiveness of sins takes up the last promise in that passage, 'for I will forgive their iniquity, and I will remember their sin no more.' The wording is not quite the same, and this makes it significant that the identical phrase 'for the forgiveness of sins' is found in Mark 1:4 to describe the effect of John's baptism but is lacking in the corresponding verse in Matthew; it looks as though Matthew has withheld the phrase in the story of John and kept it for use here. Matthew stresses that the baptism of John was a baptism 'to repentance' (Matthew 3:11; contrast Mark 1:8) and he knows that it involved confession of sin, so that it would be strange if he did not regard John's baptism as in some way symbolising and conveying forgiveness. When we look at Matthew 3:2 more closely, we may observe that the omission of the phrase 'for the forgiveness of sins' is bound up with his rephrasing of the message of John so as to show that it was essentially the same as the message of Jesus (Matthew 4:17). This suggests that Matthew did not deliberately drop the idea of forgiveness from the story of John, but rather that he saved up the phrase and used it to indicate more clearly the effects of the atoning death of Jesus.[58]

One other small change that deserves mention is that in the saying about drinking wine in the kingdom Matthew adds the words 'with you', so that Jesus associates the disciples with him in partaking of the heavenly banquet. It is again clear that the change introduced by Matthew brings out more explicitly the thought of future table fellowship between Jesus and the disciples as they share together in the heavenly feast.[59]

THE LAST SUPPER IN THE GOSPEL OF LUKE

Like Mark, Luke preserves the teaching by Jesus in which he prophesied the suffering, death and resurrection of the Son of man, and in this manner he prepares the way for the inevitable denouement of the story of the ministry of Jesus. To a greater extent than Mark he brings out the fact that the purpose of Jesus was to bring salvation to needy men and women. But he has nothing corresponding to the scene in Mark 10: 35–45 which culminates in the ransom-saying, and it has often been observed that the theology of atonement plays only a small part in the Christian preaching reported in Acts. It is thus arguable that Luke deliberately played down reference to the atoning death of Jesus in both the Gospel and Acts. According to the proponents of this view he has produced a suitably edited version of Mark 10: 35–45 in Luke 22: 24–27, in which the thought of ransom has completely disappeared, and he has produced a version of the narrative of the Last Supper in which all thought of sacrifice has disappeared (Luke 22: 15–19a); it was early scribes who found this last omission unbearable and filled out Luke's text with wording drawn from Paul's account of the Last Supper.[60]

Despite the vigour with which this case has recently been presented it will not stand up to scrutiny. The essential differences between Mark and Luke which lead to the conclusion that Mark stresses the atoning death of Jesus while Luke ignores it or deliberately suppresses it reduce to the problems surrounding Mark 10: 45 and the Supper narrative. Nowhere else in Mark is the concept of ransom and atonement by the death of Jesus present. In other words, there is not such a lot of emphasis in Mark on the concept, although there is sufficient to show that it was important for him. One may notice, incidentally, that there is no indication that any serious attempt was made to read back early church theology wholesale into the Gospels; the allusions to the death of Jesus as an atonement for sin are remarkably restrained, no doubt in keeping with the historical fact that if Jesus found it difficult to convince his disciples of the fact of his death he is unlikely to have been able to say much to them about the meaning of his death.

When we turn to Luke, we find, first of all, that he has not simply omitted Mark 10:45 but the whole paragraph of which it forms a part; in other words, it is arguable that it was the omission of the paragraph which led to the omission of the verse rather than vice versa. There is an equivalent to the whole paragraph in the short conversation in Luke 22:24–27, and it is Luke's habit to omit paragraphs in Mark when he has similar material elsewhere in his Gospel. In the present case, Luke appears to be following a separate tradition from Mark, one which did not contain Mark 10:45, and this is an adequate explanation of the omission.[61] Second, the textual argument for regarding Luke 22:19b–20 as an original part of Luke's text is very strong.[62] Once the originality of these verses is granted, it follows that Luke has one clear reference to the atoning significance of the death of Jesus over against two in Mark, and the argument that the atonement plays an insignificant part in Luke in comparison with Mark begins to look decidedly thin. When we also note the presence of traditional expressions referring to the blood of Jesus and to Jesus as God's Servant in Acts, it becomes clear that, even though Luke may not have gone out of his way to make the theology of the cross central in his work, he has certainly not suppressed it.[63]

Although, then, there is no preparation for the concept of atonement, as expressed in the Supper sayings, in the body of the Gospel, we do find an emphasis on the salvation brought by Jesus and an especial stress on the table fellowship of Jesus with sinners. Luke in fact is interested in meal-scenes (Luke 7:36–50; 11:37–54; 14:1–35), and his Gospel contains a marked extension of the Supper scene. In Mark the words of institution are immediately followed by the singing of a hymn and the departure of the company from the table, but in Luke there is an extended conversation between Jesus and his disciples which lasts for another fifteen verses, or rather eighteen if we include the prophecy of the betrayal by Judas which comes before the words of institution in Mark. Most of this sayings-material is peculiar to Luke, and Schürmann in particular has argued that for most of it Luke was dependent on a non-Marcan source in which the various sub-sections of the conversation had already been brought together.[64] We can see here perhaps a tendency to extend the element of conversation between Jesus and his disciples into the form of a farewell discourse or dialogue, a process which reaches a climax in the Gospel of John. It is open to question whether this material was originally handed down in the form of a continuous record of what was said at the Last

Supper; the fact that some of the material has parallels in other Gospel contexts (Matthew 19:28; Mark 10:35–45) may be regarded as an argument against this view. But most of the material has an inner relation to the Last Supper setting. The prophecies of the betrayal by Judas and of Simon's defection, and the final saying about the two swords cannot well belong to any other context, and the two groups of sayings about service and eating and drinking in the kingdom of the Messiah (Luke 22:24–27, 28–30) are most appropriately placed in the setting of the Last Supper. Whatever be the process of composition, Luke has brought together material that originally belonged to the Supper scene, possibly with other appropriate material, and thus given us an extended account of what took place at the Supper.

The result of this procedure is that the account of the institution of the Lord's Supper becomes part of a larger scene in which the sayings of Jesus are of decisive importance. What Jesus said, as well as what he did, at the Last Supper is significant. The words of institution take their place in a fuller group of sayings in which Jesus prepares his disciples for the future after his death. To put the point more theologically, one might say that Luke stresses the Word alongside the Sacrament, perhaps indeed more than the Sacrament.

We cannot discuss here the full content of this teaching by Jesus for its own sake, but we must note how it contributes to our understanding of the Last Supper.[65]

First, the element of betrayal which we have seen in Mark and Matthew is also present here. It is accentuated by the way in which the prophecy of betrayal follows on immediately without a break from the cup-saying, although the saying itself probably preceded the words of institution; the way in which Mark refers to the disciples dipping in the same dish with Jesus (Mark 14:20; *cf.* John 13:26) suggests that the saying took place during the earlier part of the meal.[66] The effect of this insertion is, then, to place in the strongest contrast the self-giving of Jesus in death and the act of treachery which on the human level led to his death. At the same time the strong adversative with which v. 21 begins in the Greek text has the effect of excluding the traitor from the blessings which have just been promised to the disciples, and the final comment that the disciples began to question one another as to which of them would be the traitor may not merely indicate their curiosity to know the identity of the traitor but may also convey something of the force of the question which they asked one after another in Mark's version, 'Is it I?' The Last Supper narrative thus suggests that the Lord's Supper should be an occasion for solemn and serious self-examination.

This pattern of divine promise offered amid human weakness and sinfulness continues throughout the passage. Immediately after the prophecy of the betrayal Luke records a dispute among the disciples as to which among them was the greatest. Anybody who doubts whether grown men can behave in such a childish manner can easily be provided with examples of such behaviour among politicians, academics, military men and others; heaven help the man who unwittingly takes a higher place of precedence in a procession than belongs to him! Jesus' reply draws a powerful contrast between the way of the world and the way which ought to characterise the disciples. Those who actually occupy positions of authority and leadership must conduct themselves as servants of the others. The point is clinched by a parable. Everybody admits that the 'greater' person is served at table by the 'lesser'. Let the disciples take note, then, of the example of Jesus who himself took the position of the servant. This saying suggests that Jesus used to wait on his disciples at table. Although nothing is said about his filling this role at the Last Supper, the story of the foot-washing in John 13 would provide an appropriate setting for the present saying. At the same time one may see in the saying an allusion to the 'service' which Jesus rendered his disciples in a deeper way. The sayings here are similar in content to those in Mark 10:35–45, and it is important to remember that in Mark 10:45 the thought of Jesus' service is expanded by his reference to the Son of man who came to serve and to give his life a ransom for the many. Although Luke has not recorded this part of the tradition, it brings out the fuller significance of the saying of Jesus.[67] Schürmann has suggested that the saying should also be seen as an encouragement to the disciples gathered for the Lord's Supper to serve the needy by their gifts, but this is perhaps over-subtle.[68]

In sharp contrast comes a third brief section in which Jesus speaks of the disciples as those who have persevered in following him through the trials of his ministry, and he promises them the reward of eating and drinking with him at his table in the kingdom and also of sitting on thrones as rulers of the tribes of Israel.[69] Here the thought shifts from the failures of the disciples to their faithfulness to Jesus and promises reward. It is the same motif as in Romans 8:17: 'provided we suffer with him in order that we may also be glorified with him.' What is promised is a share in the heavenly banquet, a thought which fits in with and develops the thought of eating and drinking in the coming kingdom in the core of the Supper narrative.

The two remaining sections of the narrative revert to the dangers and difficulties of the disciples. There is the warning to Simon Peter that he will deny Jesus, a warning which appears in an expanded form in Luke and contains the promise that though Satan will 'sift' the disciples in order to test their faith and cause them to fall, nevertheless Jesus has prayed for Peter that he may stand firm and be a source of strength to the others, even despite his own lapse. Finally, there is a dialogue in which Jesus again warns the disciples of the stern realities which they will face when they go out from the Supper into the harsh world; they are followers of One who will himself be regarded as a transgressor and suffer the corresponding penalty, and they cannot expect to be treated any differently. Yet they must not be tempted to respond to violence with violence; the way of Jesus is that of love and non-resistance.

This passage brings out the harsh realities that surrounded the Last Supper. Any danger of sentimentalising the situation is firmly resisted by Luke who is only too conscious of the solemn character of the scene. Luke has sometimes been attacked for presenting a 'theology of glory' rather than a 'theology of the cross'. E. Käsemann can write à propos of Luke-Acts:

> It is true that there are inescapable upsets, obstacles, menaces and even martyrdoms. Sometimes it comes to disputes within the community, and even among its leaders. But in the long run they end happily; generally speaking, all are of one mind and at least ready to compromise. The devil finds it difficult to get a living among so many godly people, and so he has to call in the services of outsiders and dishonest people ... Does not Luke idealize more than is legitimate for a historian, and even for a devotional writer? ... Even in his own time, Luke could cling to this only because he did not feel deeply enough the offence of Jesus' cross. Of course, he relates the passion story; but he makes it, like Stephen's martyrdom, a matter of a peaceful death and overcoming.'[70]

One is tempted to comment that Luke has seldom been so misrepresented. The narrative of the Last Supper is impregnated with apostasy, self-seeking, denial and betrayal, and Luke demonstrates that attendance at the supper does not transport the disciples straight to paradise, nor does it lift them out of the midst of trial and temptation and the danger of falling away. And all this is presented in the context of Jesus' own suffering and betrayal. It is a grim narrative which heightens the thought of the self-giving of Jesus and of the promise which he makes that through his death salvation and a share in the heavenly banquet are offered to weak, fickle disciples.

From all this we see that the account of the words of institution must not be considered in isolation from the rest of the Gospel story. It has a context both in the immediately surrounding events and in the ministry of Jesus as a whole, and it cannot be properly appreciated, whether historically or theologically, until it is seen in this broader context. At the same time, the three Gospels each present the narrative in their own way and their complementary witness throws further light on the significance of the Last Supper. In undertaking this study of what the Gospels say about the Last Supper we have already begun to see something of its significance for the early church. We can now proceed to look at the evidence for its continuing significance in the celebration of the Lord's Supper.

CHAPTER FIVE

The Lord's Supper in the Early Church

Our discussion so far has been concerned with the existence and character of the tradition concerning the last meal which Jesus held with his disciples before his death. Whatever the precise date and nature of that meal may have been, the tradition understood it to be a Passover meal held amid the associations of that feast for the Jews. But Jesus transformed the meal. He saw it as an occasion of fellowship with his disciples, the last occasion of this kind, and thus it took on the character of a farewell meal. At the meal Jesus distributed bread and wine to his disciples and in addition to the normal grace he spoke various sayings which gave a symbolical significance to the bread and wine. The bread was interpreted as his body or himself, given in death for 'many', *i.e.* for the people as a whole; the cup was interpreted as his blood which inaugurated a new covenant or as the covenant brought into being by his blood which was shed as a sacrificial offering on behalf of others. In this way Jesus made use of motifs from Exodus 24, Isaiah 53 and Jeremiah 31 to attach theological significance to his forthcoming death. Finally, he made it clear that this simple rite should be repeated by his disciples until they should be reunited with him in fellowship at the heavenly banquet, and in some way he regarded this rite as making up for his physical absence from them.

The early church took up this tradition, preserved it, and lived in the light of it. We now want to see what happened in the church as it followed out the command of Jesus. We have already seen how the Evangelists incorporated the tradition in their Gospels and have observed something of the significance which they attached to it. But our present concern is with the life of the church as it met together and celebrated the rite that came to be known as the Lord's Supper. One possible way to begin this examination would be by attempting to trace the history of the communal meals held by the early church in Palestine and elsewhere and to see whether we can establish how the celebration of the Lord's Supper developed. This is a question that cannot be ignored, and we must return to it in due course. It is, however, a difficult question, and therefore it may be wiser to begin from the other end, namely from the fullest account which we possess of the life of an early church in which the celebration of the Lord's Supper was causing problems. We shall, therefore, move straight from the Last Supper to the celebration of the Lord's Supper in the church at Corinth and see what we can learn about the character and significance of the meal from this source.[1]

THE LORD'S SUPPER AT CORINTH

(1). *The church meal*

From the general character of Paul's comments on the way in which the church at Corinth celebrated the Lord's Supper (1 Cor. 11: 17–34) we can assume that the Supper was held at frequent intervals, and not merely as an annual remembrance of the Lord's death at the Passover season. This view is confirmed by the evidence of Acts which shows that the church met to 'break bread' as often as daily in Jerusalem (Acts 2: 46). From 1 Corinthians 16, where we hear how the members of the church were to set aside a contribution for the church in Jerusalem on the first day of the week, it seems that the church regularly met together on that day; there is certainly no other very obvious reason as to why the members set aside their contributions on that day.[2] We may be entitled to go further and to assume that when the church met on the Sunday it was usual to hold the Lord's Supper.

The Lord's Supper was held in the context of a church meal, and it was the fact that the meal was being celebrated in what

Paul regarded as a disorderly fashion that led to its being mentioned in his letter. The problems in the church evidently arose from social differences between the members. The church contained people drawn from both the wealthy and the poorer classes, including slaves and ex-slaves. It was the custom for the participants to bring their own food and drink with them. Instead, however, of sharing them out at a common table in the manner of a modern 'pot luck supper' so that everybody could have their share of the various foodstuffs, the members each ate and drank what they themselves had brought. The wealthy brought so much food and drink that they could indulge in gluttony and even in drunkenness. The poor, however, had little or nothing to bring with the result that some of them went hungry and could not enjoy a decent meal. Paul further says that some people, presumably those who had more to eat, began eating before the others.

Thus far there would be general agreement on the facts of the situation. An attempt to explore it further has been made by G. Theissen who develops four points. First, he agrees about the difference between the wealthy and the poor; they formed two groups in the church, and this explains Paul's comment about 'divisions' in the church. When Paul talks about each person eating 'his own meal' (v. 21), Theissen takes this to be a contrast to the 'Lord's Supper' which was the common meal of bread and wine. The rich were eating 'their own' supplies of food instead of putting them at the disposal of the company as a whole. Second, contrary to the commonly held view, Theissen argues that in Corinth the breaking of the bread and the drinking of the cup were two separate acts, one at the beginning of the meal and the other at the end. Once the bread-saying had been spoken, the common meal began. What was happening was that the rich members of the congregation were starting to eat their own meals before the formal opening of the meal. Third, Theissen holds that v. 21 means 'during the meal each takes his own food', and that it signifies that during the actual communal meal the rich shared some of the bread and wine but kept back some for themselves. Social distinctions were reflected in the quantity of food consumed. Fourth, it is argued that there was also a distinction in the quality of the food. The rich brought meat, fish or other delicacies, and Theissen thinks that they did not see the need to share these since the instructions for the Lord's Supper mentioned only bread and wine as forming the common meal. Such lack of concern for the needs of the poor seen in giving them poorer quality food when they ate in the houses of their better-class neighbours can be paralleled from ancient sources. Thus in Corinth the rich, who no doubt thought that they were being charitable to the poor by opening up their houses for church meetings and by providing some food and drink for them, were in fact emphasising their social superiority over against them, and evidently felt no twinges of conscience over doing so.[3]

Theissen's case is an interesting one and helps to clarify what was going on, even if some aspects of it are speculative.[4] It is clear that Paul was shocked by what was going on and attacked the behaviour of the Corinthians quite strongly. He insisted that people who felt hungry and wanted to eat a large meal should do so at home before coming to the church gathering. It is not altogether certain whether he felt that there should be a modest common meal in church, or that there should be no meal at all beyond the morsel of bread and the mouthful of wine which were consumed in the sacramental act, but the former of these possibilities is the more likely. When the congregation came together, they should not start eating one after another as they arrived, but they should wait so that a real common meal could be held.

(2). *The Agape meal*

In Jude 12 the writer speaks of certain members of the church who are 'blemishes on your love feasts, as they boldly carouse together, looking after themselves'. The description of these people who put their own wants first and turn a church meal into an occasion for irreverent jollification is strongly reminiscent of the situation censured by Paul in 1 Corinthians. This suggests that both writers were talking about the same kind of meal. Here in Jude it is called a 'love feast', literally a 'love'. The love feast is not mentioned elsewhere in the New Testament, although the author of 2 Peter makes a punning reference to it in 2 Peter 2:13, a verse which is probably dependent on the phrase used in Jude.[5] For the next reference to it we must turn to the Epistles of Ignatius at the beginning of the second century; he rules that 'it is not lawful to baptise or hold a love feast without the bishop' (Smyrnaeans 8:2).[6] There is nothing to suggest that the love feast was a separate kind of meal from the Lord's Supper, and it seems more probable that these were two different names for the same occasion. If so, the name brings out the important point that the Lord's Supper was meant to be an occasion for Christian fellowship and love among the members of the church. During the second century the church meal and the strictly sacramental part of the meal were separated from one another and became two distinct occasions, and eventually the church meal or Agape fell into disuse. What is important is that right through the New Testament period and beyond Christians met together to hold common meals that were more than a token reception of bread and wine.[7]

(3). *The words of institution and their relevance*

It is generally thought that Paul's account implies that the sacramental partaking of the bread and the wine took place at the end of the common meal, and that the bread and wine were taken in immediate succession. This would seem to follow from the bringing together of the two acts in the liturgical formula cited by Paul and from the way in which an increasing symmetry developed in the bread and cup sayings. However, in the Lucan/Pauline form of words we are told that Jesus distributed the wine 'after supper' and from this it has been concluded that originally the church separated the bread and the wine by the common meal. Theissen, as we have already noted, holds that this practice still persisted in Corinth at the time when Paul was writing, since he thinks that Paul would not have cited a cultic formula and then deviated from its express ordering of the meal. This argument does not seem convincing. It ignores the fact that what Paul cited was not an account of what the church ought to do but a description of what Jesus did at a meal where he was governed by the order of proceedings at a Jewish festival. The church's meal was not a Passover meal, and therefore it was not bound by the Passover ritual; Christians could well take bread and wine together. It should be remembered that wine was not necessarily available every time the Lord's Supper was held. On the whole, it seems most probable that the bread and wine were taken at the beginning of the meal, and that Paul's problem was with people who started eating earlier.

Paul was concerned not simply with the social causes and consequences of the disorders in the church meal but with the theological significance of what was happening. In order to restore a sense of reverence he reminded the congregation of something which they knew already, the liturgical formula which he had handed on to the church when it was founded. It was a form of words which was regarded as authoritative in the church generally and was not Paul's own composition. The fact that he traces its origin back to 'the Lord' is a strong indication of the high authority which he ascribed to the contents of the formula. The origin of the Lord's Supper in the explicit command of Jesus as the Lord is thus emphasised. The church stands under obligation to celebrate the Supper. Not only so, but Paul is suggesting to the Corinthians that, if they bore in mind the implications of the formula, they would not be acting in the way they were.

We can take it for granted that Paul himself accepted the teaching of the formula. There is no indication that he has altered its words in any significant manner that would alter its sense. The opening words are variously ascribed to pre-Pauline tradition or to Paul himself,[8] but in either case they simply express what could be learned from the Gospel tradition regarding the Last Supper. The central content agrees basically with Luke, and we have already seen how the narrative has been shaped to tell what Jesus did and said, so that his actions and words could be an example for the church to follow. Perhaps we should be more precise and say that the formula lays down the pattern of what Jesus did at the Last Supper for the leader of the celebration of the Lord's Supper to follow. It is to be presumed that some member of the church acted as host at the Supper and performed the appropriate actions and said the appropriate words, as contained in the formula. That the formula itself was recited is possible but is not a necessary conclusion.[9] We may also note that, despite all his concern for things to be done 'decently and in order' (1 Cor. 14:40), Paul says nothing about which members of the church were entitled to lead in the celebration; it was evidently not a matter of any concern to him. We may assume that it would be one of the people who 'devoted themselves to the service of the saints', to use Paul's own rather vague term for church workers (1 Cor. 16:15); in any case, there seems to have been no dissension on the point.

Paul cites the sayings of Jesus in essentially the same form as in Luke. If we are right in claiming that Luke was not dependent upon Paul, this gives us a guarantee that Paul did not alter the wording of the sayings, and hence that he accepted their teaching without question. We can, therefore, call to mind at this point our earlier discussion of the meaning of the actions of Jesus and the bread-saying and the cup-saying, and do not need to repeat what was established then. One or two points where Paul in effect comments on the tradition will be noted later. One important element missing from the Pauline formula is Jesus' anticipation of the future meal in the kingdom of God. This is omitted because it formed no part of the interpretation of the bread and the cup. But it has an echo in Paul in v. 26 where in what seems to be his own comment on the formula he declares, 'As often as you eat this bread and drink the cup, you proclaim the Lord's death until he comes.' But the primary force of this verse lies elsewhere. It contains what Paul regarded as the point which needed most stress in Corinth. To eat and drink at the Supper is to proclaim the death of the Lord. The Supper is a memorial of Jesus in that each time it takes place it transforms the participants into preachers. The word used (*katangellō*) is one that is particularly associated with the proclamation of the gospel, and hence the Supper is an occasion and a means of preaching the good news. In this sense the Supper is a means of saving people from their sins. And the content of the saving message is the death of Jesus which is clearly in mind in the framework of the words of institution, 'on the night when he was betrayed', and in the interpretative sayings themselves. The significance of the Supper is that the bread and the cup point to the death of Jesus as a means of salvation, and thus proclaim to all who witness the Supper that Jesus died for them. This of course does not mean that it was simply the actions of distributing the elements and eating and drinking them that constituted the proclamation. The interpretative sayings constituted an essential part of the actions, so that, to use later terminology, the Word is a constitutive part of the Sacrament. We may indeed assume that a fuller verbal exposition of the gospel accompanied the essential sayings over the bread and cup, and it is not difficult to find material in the New Testament which would fit appropriately into the context of the Lord's Supper.[10]

If the significance of the Supper is, then, primarily to proclaim the death of Jesus, there is also a secondary significance in that the meal looks forward to the time when he will come again at the parousia. This phrase may well have been intended to remind the Corinthian church that it was still living in the world of temptation, weakness and sin, and was not yet in the state of glory; some of the Corinthians were evidently in danger of forgetting this basic fact (1 Cor. 4:8) and needed an injection of realism. But by proclaiming the Lord's death they were bringing nearer the day of his coming, and with it the heavenly feast.

(4). *Unworthy participation*

From this citation of the words of institution Paul draws the lesson that anybody who takes part in the Supper without thinking what he is doing and without a due sense of reverence is being irreverent towards the body and blood of Jesus. He is failing to realise that the bread and the cup represent the body and blood of Jesus or he is not taking the symbolism with sufficient seriousness. Such lack of reverence is culpable. Whoever eats and drinks in this way brings divine judgment upon himself because he does not discern the body, and therefore the members of the church should examine themselves before taking part in the meal in case they do so in a manner which is unworthy.

The phrase 'without discerning the body' (v. 29) is probably shortened for 'without discerning the body and the blood'. Nevertheless, the omission of the words 'and the blood' has led to the supposition that by 'body' Paul may here mean the church as the body of Christ rather than the crucified body of Jesus.[11] Earlier Paul had said that those who take part in the Supper are 'one body' (1 Cor. 10:16). However, it is very doubtful whether the understanding of 'body' in ch. 11 should be governed by ch. 10. Verse 29 is so close in thought to v. 27 that the term 'body' should surely be understood in the same way in both verses, and in v. 27 the linking of body and blood as counterparts to the bread and the cup makes it quite certain that we are to think of the elements as representing the crucified Lord.

Paul's language here has led to the suggestion that he has a very realistic sense of the identity of the bread and the cup with the body and blood of Jesus, and this line of thought is particularly congenial to Roman Catholic and Lutheran scholars with their insistence on the fact that the bread and wine are somehow changed into the body and blood of Jesus at the Lord's Supper.[12] We for our part may be accused of a Reformed bias, but it must be plainly stated that Paul's remarks require nothing more than a stress on the symbolism of the bread and wine and do not in any way require an identification of the bread and the wine as the body and blood of Jesus. This is particularly so if those scholars are right who insist that the body and blood of Jesus are not two separate 'parts' of the crucified Lord but each represent the whole person of Jesus. It may also be important that neither Paul nor any other New Testament writer refers to the wine as the symbol of the blood of Jesus; it is the cup which is the symbol, and the wine as such is not significant. The only mention of wine – the word itself is not used in a directly eucharistic context in the New Testament – is in the reference to 'the fruit of the vine' in Jesus' prophecy of his death and the heavenly meal which was not taken over into the Lord's Supper. Paul's thought is no different from that of Hebrews with its condemnation of the person who has 'profaned the blood of the covenant by which he was sanctified' (Heb. 10:29); in both cases the language is metaphorical.

Where Paul does enter into an area that is hard for us to comprehend is when he warns those who partake unworthily of the danger of divine judgment upon their action. He regards the bodily weakness and sickness of many in the church and the fact that some have fallen asleep in death as evidence of the Lord's judgment. A connection of this kind between sin and disease or death was certainly made in the first century (John 9:2; Jas. 5:15)[13] and Paul probably shared this view. We may observe that in Paul's view the judgment was intended for the good of those who were thus disciplined. The Lord's purpose in it was that those who suffered his judgment now might be spared from the judgment on the sinful world at the End, and thus the judgment had a deterrent and reformatory purpose. It was better still, of course, if the Corinthians were to 'judge' themselves, so that they might be spared this temporal judgment of the Lord on their sin. Paul, therefore, sees a merciful purpose in the judgment; it was intended to bring the members of the church to repentance. The moral purpose of the judgment can accordingly be defended. What is more difficult is the direct causal relationship between a sinful act and a physical penalty inflicted by the Lord: can calamities be directly associated with specific acts of sin? What Paul was doing was to give an explanation of actual events in the church; the facts were that some people were ill and some had died, and Paul interprets these calamities as judgments upon sin. It is, therefore, Paul's *interpretation* of these events which raises questions. All that we can say is that he believed that divine judgment could overtake those who participated unworthily in the sacrament; it is not a view that is generally shared in modern western Christendom which holds that, whatever may have happened in the first century, this kind of connection cannot be drawn today.[14]

Paul's words show how seriously he regarded the sin of the Corinthians. We should remind ourselves at this point that it was the lack of reverence which the Corinthians showed by their attitude to the poorer Christians among them and by their riotous behaviour at the meal which constituted their sin. Self-centredness and lack of love were the essence of their wrong conduct. This is important in any modern application of Paul's warning.

At the same time Paul may well be establishing a principle of wider application. It may well be legitimate to bring 10:22 into the discussion at this point. Despite their superstitious reverence for the sacraments as guarantees against the danger of falling into sin and under judgment, the Corinthians needed to be warned against attempting to combine the worship of idols with participation in the Lord's Supper; they may have thought of the Supper as not being essentially different from a pagan religious meal and thus failed to give the Lord his due honour. This may have been one aspect of their unworthy participation in the meal.

In some Christian circles today the fear of partaking unworthily in the Supper leads to believers of otherwise excellent character refraining from coming to the table of the Lord. When this happens, Paul's warning is being misunderstood. The Lord's Supper is the place where the forgiveness of sin is proclaimed and offered to all who would receive it. Paul's warning was not to those who were leading unworthy lives and longed for forgiveness but to those who were making a mockery of that which should have been most sacred and solemn by their behaviour at the meal. It was the high-handed sin which earned his condemnation and emphatically not the feeling of personal unworthiness. When he counsels self-examination before partaking of the meal, he is asking people to realise what it is that they are celebrating and to come to the table in an appropriate frame of mind.

(5). *Traces of an introductory liturgy*

It is possible that we should link Paul's warning about judgment here in ch. 11 with some words at the end of the Epistle. It is widely held that the closing words of 1 Corinthians form part of a Christian liturgy intended to lead into a celebration of the Supper. When the church gathered together, there would be a reading of Paul's letter as the Word of God for the occasion. At the end Paul includes phrases which may have been used in the church to introduce the next part of the proceedings. The leader would pronounce the words: 'If any one has no love for the Lord, let him be accursed. Our Lord, come.' Then would follow the blessing, 'The grace of the Lord Jesus be with you all,' followed on this particular occasion by a greeting from Paul himself: 'My love be with you all in Christ Jesus'.[15]

If this view is correct, the church pronounces a curse on those who do not love, *i.e.* hate, the Lord, and this would have special application to those who partook unworthily. It could indeed be this curse which was regarded as leading to the illness and death of some members of the church. We may compare the power attached to Peter's condemnation of Ananias and Sapphira (Acts 5:11), or the way in which Paul believed that sinful members of the church could be delivered to Satan (1 Cor. 5:3–5). Since the language here is somewhat unusual for Paul, this would support the view that a traditional formula is being cited.

Other features in the same context may also reflect the setting of the Lord's Supper. The prayer for the Lord's coming is variously interpreted as referring to his final coming at the parousia, or as a petition for his spiritual presence at the Supper. In the latter case the thought could be of a presence which could be a means of salvation or condemnation according to the spiritual state of those taking part. In our view it is most probable that the Maranatha prayer (or statement) refers to the parousia, as in Phil. 4:5 and Rev. 22:20. This view is confirmed by the eschatological hope expressed in 1 Cor. 11:25. In any case, it is fairly certain that the hope belongs to the Lord's Supper. We have already seen that such a hope may have been associated with the Jewish Passover meal. It is expressly included in a eucharistic prayer in Didache 10, and it is possible that Rev. 22:17–21 is also part of a eucharistic liturgy.[16]

In addition to the benedictions which close the Epistle, the kiss of peace which Paul directed the members of the church to give to one another was also a part of the Christian meeting and thus associated with the Lord's Supper. Here was a further sign of the love and fellowship which ought to have been demonstrated at the meal, not merely in an act of greeting but also in genuine, concrete sharing and caring for one another.

(6). *Idolatrous feasts and the Lord's Supper*

We must now retrace our steps in the Epistle to some earlier teaching which is of fundamental importance for Paul's understanding of the Supper. We may briefly note in passing Paul's reference to the sacrifice of Christ as the Christian paschal lamb and his exhortation to the church to celebrate the feast in sincerity and truth (1 Cor. 5:7f.). This is most plausibly taken as a reference to the forthcoming celebration of Easter as the feast corresponding to the Jewish Passover, but we have no further information about the nature of such a celebration.[17]

The passage to which we must devote our main attention is ch. 10. The situation envisaged here is that the church at Corinth contained some members who thought that they had reached a high level of spirituality and stood in no danger of condemnation. Paul was only too conscious that they were deluding themselves. There was a cliquish spirit in the church, leading some of the members to rank themselves behind different human leaders and bicker with one another; there were some cases of rank immorality, with members of the church guilty of sexual immorality, greed, idolatry, profanity, drunkenness and robbery, and the other members of the church were prepared to tolerate the continuance of these sins of their pre-conversion days. In particular, Paul was aware of the temptations posed by the way in which some of the members took part in idolatrous rites, specifically the eating of meals in pagan temples. Paul was not too worried about Christians eating food which had been sacrificed to idols and was then offered for sale in the shops or served up at table in the house of some pagan friend (1 Cor. 10:25–30). He knew well that offering meat to an idol could not affect it in any way and make it a cause of defilement for a Christian who recognised the emptiness of idol-worship, although he recognised that not all Christians shared this viewpoint and insisted that so-called 'strong' Christians must not act in a way that was unhelpful to these so-called 'weak' Christians. But taking part in meals in honour of a pagan god with their concomitant temptations to idolatry and immorality was a different matter. It looks as though some of the Corinthians regarded themselves as protected from any kind of spiritual danger at such occasions by their participation in the sacraments of baptism and the Lord's Supper. They may well have regarded the sacraments as having some kind of quasi-magical prophylactic power such as was ascribed to them at later stages in church history. It was an attitude of this kind that Paul felt it necessary to combat vigorously.

He commenced his argument by reminding his readers that the people of Israel had certain 'types' or foreshadowings of the Christian sacraments in their wanderings through the wilderness. They had been 'baptised' in a manner of speaking by travelling under the cloud and passing through the sea with Moses, and they had enjoyed spiritual food and drink. They had eaten manna provided by God, and they had drunk water from the rock, a rock which Paul saw as a 'type' of Jesus Christ. This remarkable passage is our justification for linking together baptism and the Lord's Supper as two events of the same kind, to which the common name of 'sacraments' has come to be given. The fact that Paul speaks of 'spiritual' food and drink enjoyed by the Israelites in the wilderness suggests that he thought of the bread and the cup of wine in the Lord's Supper as being also spiritual food and drink. But the 'spiritual' character of the manna and the water lay not in any special nature which they possessed as compared with other physical foods but rather in the fact that they were supplied by God. This point is perhaps significant. We cannot argue from this parallel that Paul thought that the bread and wine were identical with Christ himself, but rather that Christ was regarded as the source of the blessings which the church enjoys. Another possibility is that the manna and water were regarded as 'spiritual' in that they foreshadowed the spiritual food given to Christians.[18] However, in that the food and drink were miraculously provided by God, they could have been regarded as somehow conveying a divine blessing and power, and Paul's point was that, whatever virtue the food and drink possessed, they were no prophylactic against spiritual danger. The Israelites fell into sin and perished as a result in the wilderness. Paul was warning the Corinthians that their participation in baptism and the Lord's Supper was no guarantee against the possibility of them succumbing to temptation and coming under divine judgment. 'Strong' Christians who felt that they were able to withstand any temptation should beware.

Paul applied this point specifically to taking part in feasts which involved the worship of idols. 'Strong' Christians could claim that since idols were non-existent they could take part in their empty and meaningless rites with impunity. Paul, however, disputed this, since in his view demonic powers were at work in idolatrous rites.

In order to make this point he drew the attention of the readers to the implications of two parallel sayings, which may well be based on tradition:[19] 'The cup of blessing which we bless, is it not a participation in the blood of Christ? The bread which we break, is it not a participation in the body of Christ?' (1 Cor. 10:16). The unusual order of the cup and the bread here has led to speculations about eucharistic rites with an inverted order of the elements,[20] but undoubtedly the reason for the inversion is that Paul deliberately reversed the order of the sayings because he wanted to make a point about the bread rather than about the cup.[21] Paul's language shows that he is dependent on a tradition which reflected the origins of the Lord's Supper in a Jewish meal. The cup of blessing was a Jewish technical term for the cup of wine for which a blessing, *i.e.* thanksgiving, was given to God. The idea that the cup was blessed rather than God is one that dies hard and has been used to justify some kind of 'consecration' of the elements in modern liturgies whereby they become vehicles of divine blessing to those who receive them. But 1 Corinthians 14:16 shows that by 'bless' Paul meant the giving of thanks to God, and this fits in with the Jewish practice of blessing God for his gifts of food and drink. When 1 Timothy 4:4f. refers to the consecration of food by thanksgiving, through the word of God and prayer, this refers not to any special consecration of the eucharistic elements, but to the fact that all foods are 'clean' for believers who accept them gratefully as God's gifts; they cannot be rendered 'unclean' and religiously defiling by the say-so of heretics.[22]

What the statements cited by Paul show is that the cup is a means of participation in the blood of Jesus, and the bread is a means of participation in his body. Alternatively, Paul may mean that to share in the cup and the bread is to share in the blood and body of Jesus. Either way, the word 'participation' or 'communion', as it has been traditionally rendered, implies receiving, along with other Christians, a share in the blood and body of Jesus. It is obvious that Paul s thoughts here are far from any suggestion of 'eating the deity', something which would have been totally foreign to his Jewish way of thinking. Rather, 'Paul is thinking of the share all Christians enjoy, and enjoy together, in the benefits secured for them through the blood of Christ. The whole expression means "that the Christian through taking the wine in the cup, receives an interest in the death of Christ, which, according to Rom. iii.25; v.9, mediates to man the justification and atonement God provides" (Kümmel).'[23]

This explanation is preferable to that offered by F. Hauck who thinks that the reference is to fellowship with Jesus: 'Thus the nature of the Lord's Supper is expounded by Paul in terms of fellowship with the person of Christ, namely κοινωνία with His body and blood (v. 16). For Paul the bread and wine are vehicles of the presence of Christ, just as the Jewish altar is a pledge of the presence of God. Partaking of bread and wine is union (sharing) with the heavenly Christ.'[24] This explanation is faulty in that it confuses 'participation in' with 'sharing with'; it also draws a false analogy from Paul's mention of the altar in v. 18; and it is reduced to saying that Paul could have made his point simply by reference to the body of Jesus, as his whole person, but had to introduce a somewhat superfluous reference to his blood simply because it was mentioned in the traditional formula. It is much more probable, then, that Paul is thinking of Christians as sharing in the benefits of the Lord's passion, and so becoming his people. The thought of fellowship with the Lord arises out of sharing in a meal which he has provided and at which he is the host (see below).

Paul's next statement is at first sight difficult to follow. He argues: 'Because there is one bread, we who are many are one body, for we all partake of the one bread'. This comment on the traditional wording in the previous verse indicates that at the Lord's Supper one loaf of bread was broken up and shared among the members, in the same way as one cup was distributed among them. Paul draws the conclusion from this practice that those who share the one loaf broken into many pieces are thereby joined together in the unity represented by the original loaf, and so he can speak of them as constituting one body. Here Paul must be using 'body' in a non-technical sense to refer not to the physical or heavenly body of Jesus but to the church; it is his first use of a metaphor which is developed later in ch. 12 when he speaks of believers becoming members of one body by baptism and having their several different functions in the unified working of the whole body. Since Paul can refer to the church as 'the body of Christ' (1 Cor. 12:27), it is obvious that some confusion could arise with the crucified body of Jesus, especially since the loaf of bread at the Supper could represent both, and it is perhaps not surprising that some modern theologians have added to the confusion by claiming that the crucified and risen body of Jesus is identical with the church.[25]

But why does Paul make this statement? It seems to break up the flow of his argument. It may in fact be a parenthetical comment,[26] but it is important for Paul's general position. Throughout this section of the letter Paul is discussing not only the personal dangers faced by 'strong' Christians but also their responsibility lest by their example they lead astray and plunge into sin and judgment their brothers 'for whom Christ died' (1 Cor. 8:11) and so act as stumbling blocks to the church of God (1 Cor. 10:32). Paul's present point, then, is that Christians are bound together with their fellow-Christians in the Lord's Supper and must express that unity in love and consideration for others.[27]

The main argument about the position of the 'strong' Christians themselves is resumed in v. 18. Paul draws their attention to the routine followed at Jewish sacrifices. At certain offerings, such as the peace offering or the Passover, the Israelites who made a sacrifice to God ate parts of the meat which had been offered up to God. In this way, says Paul, they became 'partners in the altar'. Later on, in v. 20, Paul speaks of being 'partners with demons', and implies that by analogy Christians are 'partners with God'. Hence it has been argued that in the present statement the altar stands by metonymy for 'God'.[28] But it is doubtful whether this is the meaning. It is more likely that Paul means 'sharers in the benefits arising from the sacrifices offered on the altar'.[29] This interpretation is supported by a passage from Philo who says that when a sacrifice has been offered the meat becomes the property of God, and he makes 'the convivial company of those who carry out the sacrifices partners of the altar whose board they share' (Philo, Spec. Leg. 1:221). Philo means that God invites the worshippers to a feast at which he is the host and the provider of good things. Thus the people who eat the sacrifices are partakers of the food from the altar of the God whom they worship, and in this sense they enjoy fellowship with God at the meal.[30]

Now, says Paul, although idols are unreal and food sacrificed to idols is not really different from ordinary food, yet offerings made on pagan altars are not made to the true God; they must, then, be offerings to demons. Here, incidentally, Paul is denying that worship offered to idols is really worship offered to God in ignorance of his real identity.[31] Hence the people who take part in pagan worship are offering sacrifices to demons and eating food belonging to demons; in this way they are entering into a relationship of fellowship or partnership with demons. Paul may be implying that to do so is to come under the evil power of demons, but his explicit point is that this practice cannot be combined with attending the Lord's Supper. For in the same way the person who takes part in the Supper is entering into fellowship with God, a God who is jealous of his people and who will not tolerate a divided loyalty between himself and demons. One cannot drink the cup of the Lord and the cup of demons or eat at the table of the Lord and the table of demons. This thought may well be present in Paul's later comments on what it means to partake of the Supper in an unworthy fashion.

It will be clear from what Paul has said that he does not think of the Lord's Supper as itself a sacrifice in any sense of the term, despite a long history of Christian interpretation to the contrary.[32] The Supper is likened not to a sacrifice at an altar but to the meal which follows the sacrifice and which is celebrated with a table and a cup. Furthermore, the sacrifice is that of Jesus on the cross, the sacrifice provided by God himself, which is incapable of repetition and which cannot be offered by men. To come to the Lord's Table is to come at his invitation to share in the benefits of the sacrifice of Jesus at Calvary, and the bread and the cup are the symbols of that sacrifice. At the Supper, then, the participants have fellowship with God as their host because it is his table and he provides the spiritual blessings (*cf.* 1 Cor. 10:4). But this communion with God is not the same thing as participation in the body and blood of Jesus, and it is not achieved through eating bread and drinking wine in the sense that we somehow partake of Christ or of God in so doing. Rather, Paul begins from the fact that at the Supper eating the bread and drinking the cup signify that we receive all the benefits of Christ's death, goes on to argue that these are the blessings of the meal that follows an act of sacrifice, and claims that those who take part in such a meal enjoy fellowship with the Lord.

Although Paul's main purpose in this chapter was to lay a foundation for his warning to so-called 'strong' Christians against thinking that the Christian sacraments could protect them from falling under judgement because of their sin and that they could cheerfully participate in pagan sacrifices, he has at the same time laid bare something of his understanding of the Lord's Supper and its significance. It emerges that he regarded the Lord's death as a sacrifice, and elsewhere he shows that he thought of it as a sin-offering bringing about reconciliation between God and mankind (Rom. 3:24f.). Second, he regarded the cup and the bread as means of participation in the benefits of that sacrifice. The person who takes part in the meal with its dramatic reminder of the death of Jesus knows what it means to be justified and to have peace with God. It goes without saying that faith was an essential element in such participation. Third, he saw the Supper as a meal in which the Lord was host and thus one in which believers were brought into communion and union with him.

THE 'BREAKING OF BREAD' IN ACTS

When we turn from Paul to Luke, we find ourselves faced by a somewhat different description of the practice of the early Christians. We shall first of all present the picture given by

Luke, and then we must ask what can be learned from it regarding the practice of the early church.

(1). *The post-resurrection meals with Jesus*

The picture which Luke gives to us in Acts was intended to be read by people who were already familiar with the contents of his Gospel. We have already discussed Luke's account of the Last Supper and seen that it stands in a Gospel which devotes more attention than the others to the meals at which Jesus was present.[33] But there remains some further material which is of the utmost significance for our investigation. Luke describes how on more than one occasion there were appearances of the risen Jesus in which he met with his disciples and they partook of food together.

The first, and the most striking, of these accounts is that of the two disciples journeying to Emmaus who were joined by a stranger whom at first they did not recognise. During their journey they fell into conversation in which the two disciples spoke about the recent death of Jesus and related how this had dashed their hopes that this prophet might have been the deliverer of Israel; the reports that his tomb had been found empty and that some of the women in the band of his disciples had seen a vision of angels who declared that he was alive had done nothing to encourage them but had simply added to their confusion. Then the stranger proceeded to instruct them from the Scriptures that the Messiah was meant to suffer before entering into his glory. The conversation lasted until towards the end of the day they reached their destination and invited the stranger to stay with them for the night. Then 'when he was at table with them, he took the bread and blessed, and broke it, and gave it to them' (Luke 24:30). It was at this point that the veil fell from the eyes of the two disciples and they recognised who the stranger was. No sooner had they done so, however, than he vanished from their sight.

The significance of this episode is important. First of all, the description of the action of Jesus is strongly reminiscent of the stories of the feeding of the multitude[34] and of the Last Supper. Whether or not the two disciples in this story were present at the Last Supper – and Luke implies that they had not been present at it – the readers of the Gospel were intended to see that what Jesus did at mealtimes, and especially at the Last Supper, enabled the disciples to recognise who he was. Hence they told their friends back at Jerusalem 'how he was known to them in the breaking of the bread' (Luke 24:35). So far as the present story is concerned, the breaking of bread revealed the identity of the stranger who was visibly present with them. Second, we must note that the description is purely of the breaking and distribution of the bread; none of the distinguishing features of the Last Supper are mentioned, no wine, no words of interpretation. Third, the effect of the revelation of the stranger's identity was to make the disciples say, 'Did not our hearts burn within us while he talked to us on the road, while he opened to us the scriptures?' (Luke 23:32), and when they returned to Jerusalem they related 'what had happened on the road'. This makes it clear that the elation experienced by the disciples was not simply at the breaking of the bread but already during his conversation with them on the road while he expounded the scriptures. The reality of the risen Jesus was already being experienced by the disciples as he spoke to them, but was recognised for what it was only after the visual revelation of Jesus at the breaking of bread. That is to say, the disciples experienced Jesus as the risen Lord both in his exposition of the Scriptures to them and in his breaking of the bread to them, and Luke intends his readers to see that these two things belong together.[35]

A second scene follows directly afterwards in which the risen Lord appears to the disciples gathered together in Jerusalem. On this occasion Jesus himself actually eats a piece of broiled fish in the presence of the disciples. There is, however, no mention of the disciples sharing in the meal with him, even if we may presuppose that they were gathered together for a meal when he appeared and that they gave him what was to hand on the table to eat. The emphasis is not on a meal enjoyed by the disciples with Jesus, but rather on the evidential value of the action of Jesus in demonstrating to them that he was not a ghost but a resurrected man (Luke 24:36–43). Once again, however, we have the element of the Lord's instruction of the disciples from the Scriptures as an essential part of his revelation of himself to them (Luke 24:44–49).

There are two references in Acts to occasions such as these. The first is in Acts 1:4 where we are told how Jesus spoke with the disciples while he was eating with them (RSV mg). The meaning of the word translated 'eating' is not altogether clear but it most probably refers to table fellowship of some kind.[36] Here again, then, we have the conjunction of instruction by the risen Lord with table fellowship with him. The second reference

is in Peter's sermon in the house of Cornelius where he tells
how the apostles were chosen by God to be witnesses to the
resurrection and in this capacity they 'ate and drank with him
after he rose from the dead. And he commanded us to preach
to the people' (Acts 10:41f.).

These references show that Luke regarded the resurrection
appearances of Jesus as including occasions when he ate with his
disciples and taught them. One of these occasions is described
in terms reminiscent of the feeding of the multitude and of the
Last Supper and is described as the 'breaking of bread'. Luke's
description of the resurrection appearances in these terms is
certainly not invention. It is independently attested by the story
of the resurrection appearance in John 21:9–14 which tells of the
breakfast by the Sea of Tiberias where Jesus and the disciples
ate bread and fish together. We can be sure that Luke's account
of such meals is based on tradition.[37] What emerges from the
account, as Luke gives it, is that there is some connection between
the earlier stories of Jesus eating with his disciples and the
stories of his eating with them after his resurrection. The meals
after the resurrection are intended to be seen as a continuation
of the fellowship with Jesus that the disciples enjoyed before
his death. At the resurrection appearances Jesus is visibly and
indeed physically present with the disciples, although it is possible for them not to recognise him and for him to come and go
suddenly in a miraculous fashion. We may well suspect that
Jesus, as presented in these stories, was preparing the disciples
for further occasions when his presence would still be with them
but not in a visible or tangible manner. At the same time, it is
becoming evident that the exposition of the Scriptures and the
breaking of bread are the modes by which the presence of the
risen Jesus is known.

(2). *The Breaking of Bread*

These considerations have paved the way for us to approach
the evidence in Acts. In Acts 2:42 Luke describes the activity
of those who responded to Peter's preaching on the Day of
Pentecost and were baptised. 'They devoted themselves to the
apostles' teaching and fellowship, to the breaking of bread and
the prayers.' This brief description is followed by a further
summary of the life of the early church: 'day by day, attending
the temple together and breaking bread in their homes, they
partook of food with glad and generous hearts, praising God
and having favour with all the people.' These two descriptions

are probably to be regarded as two separate items, the first telling what happened to the new converts, the second giving a more general description of the activities of the church as a whole.[38]

Opinions differ as to whether v. 42 is a description of four separate activities or of four constituent parts of an early Christian gathering, but I am inclined to agree with the latter view, provided that it is not interpreted too rigidly of a set pattern that permitted no deviations.[39] If we adopt this view, we find that the gatherings of the early Christians included teaching about the faith given in the early days in Jerusalem by the apostles themselves and doubtless inspired by the teaching of Jesus during his earthly ministry. Second, if we may take the items in a different order from Luke's, there was prayer to God, which J. Jeremias regards as the closing item in a Christian meeting; this suggestion would not of course exclude the likelihood of prayer earlier in the gathering. Third, there is what Luke calls 'fellowship'. This word could refer to the common sharing of goods which was practised by the early church (Acts 2:44f.), or it might refer to the inward bond between Christians enjoying fellowship with Christ and with one another, but it is perhaps more likely that it refers to the holding of a common meal.[40] If this interpretation is correct, then we must distinguish from this meal the 'breaking of bread' which is the fourth item on the list. We have already discovered that this term was used in the Gospels for the action of Jesus at the feeding of the multitude and at the Last Supper. It refers to the action at the opening of a meal, the action which Jesus had invested with special significance for his disciples. Here, then, we have a reference to the celebration of the Lord's Supper. If this interpretation is correct, the common meal is here distinguished from the breaking of bread, and we would have the same picture as in 1 Corinthians where the Lord's Supper proper took place in the context of a fuller meal held by the congregation.

It can of course be claimed that the picture of a Christian meeting given here reflects the practice of Luke's time and does not necessarily go back right to the beginning of the Christian church in Jerusalem. It could then be argued that the distinction between the church meal and the breaking of bread is not as early as Luke makes out. On the other hand, it must be noted that this distinction is as early as Paul's mission to Corinth and that the terminology used by Luke appears to be primitive. With all due caution we can say that the first Christians met in order to celebrate meals together and that an essential element in the meal was the ritual of the breaking of bread.

It is at this point that we can bring into our discussion the comparative material which we mentioned earlier. We saw that Jewish groups such as the Pharisees and the Qumran sect met together for meals which had a religious dimension and that the same was true of various pagan cults. There was nothing strange in religious groups holding common meals together. Now there was nothing in the accounts of the Last Supper to lead us to suppose that any of these Jewish types of meal provided the pattern for Jesus' behaviour on that occasion; on the contrary, we found that the Passover meal provided a fully adequate setting for the Last Supper. But when we come to the gatherings of Jesus' followers after the resurrection, it is very likely that the practice of other Jewish and even pagan groups in meeting together for meals encouraged them to do the same; at the same time, of course, they were carrying on the practice of meals together which had been part of their life with Jesus during his ministry.

Let us now pass in review the remainder of the evidence from Acts. The verse which we have just been considering is followed immediately by a summary of the life of the early church which describes something of the public impact upon the people of Jerusalem and also of the nature of the Christian community (Acts 2:43–46). Luke mentions their attendance at the temple, which was the centre of prayer and worship for the Jewish people,[41] and also their gathering to break bread in their own homes and to eat with joy. This extremely compact description establishes clearly enough that the Christian meetings took place in their own homes, which is what we would naturally expect, since they had no other buildings for the purpose, and that they took place daily. It also appears that the breaking of bread and the partaking of food went together. We have, then, the same picture as in v. 42 of gatherings for meals, with which the breaking of bread was associated. The new element here is the stress on the joy and sincerity of heart which was manifested in these gatherings. This joy expressed itself in praising God. Luke does not explain the precise cause of the joy. It was no doubt the expression of the new experience of salvation, and it arose out of believing in God through Jesus (Acts 16:34; *cf.* 8:39) and through the experience of the gift of the Spirit (Acts 13:52). In the light of the Emmaus story we may well feel that the experience of the presence of the risen Lord was a determinative factor (*cf.* Luke 24:41), and it has often been suggested that this was the decisive element in the meals described in Acts.[42] However, it may be worth emphasising that this point is not made explicitly in Acts and remains a matter of inference. We should, therefore, be wary of asserting that the post-resurrection meals in Acts were primarily occasions for celebrating the presence of the risen Lord; to say this is to run beyond the evidence.

A somewhat modified form of this view has been suggested by J. Wanke who claims that in the meal scenes in Acts the Lord himself is to be seen as active in saving and preserving his people.[43] This element is found in Acts 2:47, but it is not exactly a compelling association of ideas. Wanke finds stronger evidence in the story of the meeting at Troas in Acts 20:7–12. Here we have a Christian meeting which takes place on the first day of the week,[44] at which the Christians celebrate the breaking of bread. The meeting went on for a long time, as Paul had much to say on this farewell occasion, but eventually past midnight Paul concluded his remarks and broke bread and ate with the disciples. It has been suggested that this was merely the ritual of breaking of bread without an accompanying church meal, but this is unlikely since Christians were not likely to wait so long for a meal.[45] However, the language used indicates a meal, and Luke's point is precisely that the congregation was so eager to hear Paul that it was prepared to wait until past midnight before partaking of food. Even after the meal Paul still conversed with the Christians until day break when he had to depart. The picture here thus fully confirms our earlier conclusions. Within the framework of this scene Luke tells the story of the young man called Eutychus who fell from a window and was taken up dead, but was restored by Paul. Wanke draws out the point that the Lord's protection was with his people gathered for the meal, and claims that the Pauline 'Do not be alarmed' was intended to be seen by Luke's readers as a pledge of the Lord's saving power to his people.

The third reference to breaking of bread in Acts to which Wanke draws attention is the incident on the storm-tossed voyage to Malta when Paul persuaded his companions to cease fasting and take some nourishment (Acts 27:33–36). After fourteen days without food Paul felt it right to urge the crew and passengers to eat both for the sake of their own good and also as a sign of hope that they would not come to any disaster; the presupposition may well be that they had been fasting as an accompaniment to prayers for safety. 'When he had said this, he took bread, and giving thanks to God in the presence of all he

broke it and began to eat. Then they were all encouraged and
ate some food themselves.' The linking of the meal with the
thought of God's saving-power is strong, especially in v. 34
where the word translated 'strength' in RSV is the same word
as 'salvation'. What is dubious is whether a Christian 'breaking
of bread' is being described. Paul's actions are described like
those of Jesus when feeding the multitude, celebrating the Last
Supper and sitting at table with the disciples journeying to
Emmaus. Luke could then be describing the Breaking of Bread
as celebrated by Paul and his Christian companions on the ship.
However, the actions do not go beyond those of a normal
Jewish meal, and it is held openly in the presence of a mixed
company of people. In our view it is unlikely, therefore, that a
Christian sacrament is being described. What we have is an
ordinary meal shared by Paul with his friends which served as an
example to encourage the others on board ship to eat also. Nevertheless, the language which is used by Luke is probably
deliberately intended to remind his readers of the meals held by
Jesus and of the Breaking of Bread in the church and so to
suggest that something of the associations of the church's meal
were present. The meal is one in which the saving and sustain-
ing power of God is acknowledged and praise and thanks are
offered to him for his goodness.[46]

The evidence which we have considered shows that Acts
testifies to the celebration of the Breaking of Bread, apparently
in the context of a church meal. The meal itself was a joyful
occasion, celebrated at frequent intervals and as often as daily in
the early days of the church in Jerusalem. It took place in the
context of the display of God's saving power in Jesus. Although
the point is not developed in Acts, the evidence of the Emmaus
story suggests that the meal with the accompanying apostolic
teaching was regarded as an occasion when the Lord was
especially present.

(3). *Two types of church meal?*

When we compare the description in Acts with what we have
learned from Paul, some points of difference emerge. There is
no mention in Acts of a particular association of the meal with the
Last Supper. The use of wine is not mentioned, and there are
no 'words of institution'. There is no reference backwards to the
death of Jesus nor forwards to his return and to the heavenly
banquet. The meals in Acts are remarkably untheological The
emphasis is rather on the joy associated with salvation and this

may be linked, admittedly with some caution, with the presence of the risen Lord.

These differences have led to a number of related theories suggesting that there were two differing types of meal celebration in the early church. H. Lietzmann put forward the view that there was a type of meal, associated with the early church in Jerusalem, which was essentially a continuation of the meals held by Jesus with his disciples before his resurrection; at this meal the church spoke a blessing over the bread, drank from the cup of blessing, and looked forward to the return of the Lord. Over against this type of meal Lietzmann placed that of the Pauline churches which was modelled on the Last Supper and was a solemn memorial of the death of Jesus. From these two different types of meal Lietzmann traced two lines of development in the early church, the former being seen especially in the Didache and in Egyptian forms of the liturgy, and the latter in the liturgy of Hippolytus.[47]

A variant of this view was offered by E. Lohmeyer who distinguished between a Galilean form of meal and a Jerusalem form. The former corresponded essentially to Lietzmann's Jerusalem type of meal, while the latter corresponded to the Pauline type. The difference is that Lohmeyer held that both types of meal go back to the early church, since Galilean and Jerusalem Christians were in close contact with one another.[48]

A somewhat different direction was followed by O. Cullmann who argued that behind the joyful meals in Acts there lay the post-resurrection meals of Jesus with his disciples. There was a continuity between the post-resurrection meals and the celebrations of the early church, and it was the belief in the presence of the risen Lord which made them joyful occasions. It was Paul who saw the link between these meals and the Last Supper and introduced the form of the Lord's Supper in which the death of the Lord was remembered.[49]

The tensions in the text which have led to these theories are still felt by some scholars.[50] It is, however, very questionable whether the theories are tenable and necessary.[51] Various arguments can be brought against them. First, A. J. B. Higgins has observed that in order to support his theory Lietzmann had to argue that Paul's understanding of the Lord's Supper was derived from his own private and direct revelation from the Lord and was not the common property of other Christians. In Higgins' view this hypothesis of a private revelation to Paul is quite untenable. It rests on an improbable understanding of

1 Corinthians 11:23 and also it fails to do justice to the evidence which has been assembled for the Palestinian origin of the narrative of the Last Supper. It is quite impossible that the tradition which Paul cites was known only to him.

Second, the alleged antithesis between joyful celebrations of the Lord's presence and solemn memories of his death is a false one. On the one hand, the note of joy is present in the Pauline tradition in the expectation of the Lord's coming. We may also note that the thought of present communion with the Lord as the giver of the feast is found in 1 Corinthians 10, and that the selfish exuberance displayed by some of the members of the church at the meal in Corinth suggests that they failed completely to realise the solemn features of the Supper on which Paul laid stress. On the other hand, we have noted that a direct connection expressed in Acts itself, although we may well believe that such a link is implied by the Emmaus story. Further, B. Reicke has noted how in the Testaments of the Twelve Patriarchs the farewell meals of the dying patriarchs are celebrated amid great rejoicings.[52]

Third, the differences between Acts and Paul virtually disappear under analysis. The lack of wine in Acts corresponds with the fact that it was not universally available, and we have seen that the Pauline account of the words of institution may well imply that a celebration *sub una* was known in the Pauline churches. It has sometimes been thought that the term 'breaking of bread' refers to a different rite from the Lord's Supper, but it is more probable that Luke retains a Palestinian name for the Lord's Supper; if our understanding of Acts 2:42 is correct, the Breaking of Bread is to be distinguished from the fellowship meal held by the early Christians. The real problem boils down to the lack of mention of the death of Jesus in the accounts of the meals in Acts. But this is not really a problem. We have in fact only four references to such occasions in Acts, and they take the form of reports that such meals were held rather than descriptions of how the meals were held. The reader who has already become acquainted with the Gospel of Luke with its descriptions of the occasions on which Jesus broke bread should not need to be told the significance of the occasions in Acts when the disciples broke bread, especially when he remembered the command of Jesus at the Last Supper, 'Do this in remembrance of me'. Luke has provided the theological interpretation of the Breaking of Bread in advance of the occasion, and he was content simply to report that the early church celebrated the feast. We may compare, on the one hand, how he leaves us tantalisingly uncertain about the conduct of a Christian baptism, and, on the other hand, how Paul himself would have told us nothing about the theological significance of the Lord's Supper if he had not been compelled to do so by the situation in Corinth. There is, in short, nothing remarkable about Luke's silence concerning the memorial aspects of the Lord's Supper in Acts, and accordingly the major reason for distinguishing between two types of meal in the early church completely disappears. [53]

We can, then, regard Luke's account of the practice of the early church in Acts as providing a complement to Paul's understanding of the Supper, as a result of which certain valuable additions are made to the picture. Above all, Luke's contribution is to stress that the Lord's Supper is the joyous celebration of the experience of salvation in the presence of the risen Lord.

THE ABSENCE OF THE LAST SUPPER FROM THE GOSPEL OF JOHN

The last meal of Jesus with his disciples is certainly not missing from the Gospel of John. We have a full-length description of it in John 13, but the essential elements that gave the impetus to the early church to celebrate the Lord's Supper are missing. John shares various other features with the other Gospels. The last meal of Jesus is held in a Passover setting, although chronologically before the Passover. The thought of service by Jesus, expressed in the after-supper dialogue in Luke, finds significant and emphatic expression in the story of the foot-washing. John shares with the other Gospels the prophecy of the betrayal by Judas and the denial by Peter. Finally, the teaching given by Jesus is extended from its comparatively brief form in Luke to a full-length farewell discourse. The presence of these common features makes the absence of the eucharistic details all the more remarkable. Why has John omitted what we would regard as the central part of the story if we follow the synoptic presentation?

We can surely dismiss the possibility that John was ignorant of the institution of the Lord's Supper. Such lack of knowledge would be totally inexplicable. A second possibility is that John wished to keep the institution of the Supper as a secret from outsiders who might read his Gospel. [54] This theory too seems quite implausible to me, since elsewhere John is remarkably open about the teaching of Jesus in comparison with the other

Gospels. A third view is that John was opposed to the sacraments and deliberately refrained from all reference to them. Those who adopt this view are forced to explain away the obvious references to the sacraments elsewhere in the Gospel by one means or another, for example, as additions by an ecclesiastically-minded editor who wanted to bring the Gospel into conformity with orthodox Christian teaching.[55] This view breaks down on the utter artificiality of the means used to sustain it, and it can be put aside.

One such alleged redactional addition is John 6:51–58, a passage which contains language that sounds uncommonly like sacramental language. When we read, for example, 'The bread which I shall give for the life of the world is my flesh' (John 6:51), it is hard not to hear an echo in Johannine style of something like 'This (bread) is my body given for many.' Have we, then, in John 6 what might be regarded as John's equivalent to the words of institution of the Lord's Supper, and, if so, what is it doing in this unusual context?

The setting of this teaching by Jesus is a synagogue discourse which followed the miracle of feeding the multitude, a story which came to be told in language suggestive of the Last Supper in the synoptic Gospels. John's version of the story is not any more eucharistic than the other accounts. The most obviously 'eucharistic' feature is the reference in John 6:23 which describes how the boats came 'near the place where they ate the bread after the Lord has given thanks', but the originality of the cruncial phrase 'after the Lord had given thanks' in the text of the Gospel is somewhat doubtful.[56] If we accept it as original, the rather odd phraseology would seem to be intended not so much to make a eucharistic allusion as to call attention to the miracle which followed the Lord's giving of thanks (*cf.* John 11:41f.). A further feature is the Passover setting of the miracle and the discourse, which could be reminiscent of the last Passover in the ministry of Jesus, but appears rather to be the appropriate chronological setting for an exposition by Jesus which takes up themes associated with the Exodus from Egypt.

The discourse itself is punctuated by various interlocutions from the audience. In the lengthy section which runs as far as v. 51, where there is an interruption from the audience, the theme of Jesus is a contrast between perishable bread, the kind provided in the feeding miracle, and that which is imperishable and conveys spiritual life. In a second contrast this spiritual bread is compared with the manna provided by Moses in the wilderness, which was still merely food for the body despite its divine origin. The true bread of God is the person who comes down from heaven and gives life to the world, namely Jesus himself. But the effect of the contrast between Jesus and the manna is to bring out the important point that it is Jesus as the messenger of the Word or Wisdom of God who offers life. Jewish exegesis regarded the manna as a type of the Word or the Wisdom of God, and it is fairly certain that in this discourse Jesus himself is to be seen in the light of this Jewish understanding of the manna. He is the Word and Wisdom of God, and consequently it is his words which give life (John 6:63). Hence the appropriate metaphor to use for coming to Jesus and believing his words is to eat the bread which gives life (John 6:50f.). The equation of believing and eating is clear from a comparison of vs. 47 and 51; at the same time v. 35 suggests that coming to Jesus is tantamount to eating, and believing is tantamount to drinking. These equations show that language is used in a fairly plastic manner in this discourse, and this fact prepares us for a further extension of speech in v. 51c when Jesus states, 'the bread which I shall give for the life of the world is my flesh'.

Although v. 51c belongs to the preceding part of the discourse, and the break in thought comes with the question of the Jews which follows it and introduces the further comments of Jesus, it has become customary with many scholars to see a break in composition between v. 51b and 51c, and to argue that 6:51c–58 is a later interpolation in the chapter by a redactor with sacramental interests.[57] A discussion of this point is hardly in place here, and we must be content to comment that the arguments for an interpolation have not convinced a number of significant commentators, and that we regard their judgment as sound.[58]

The point of v. 51c is that Jesus is going to give his own flesh for the life of the world. This cannot be understood in any other way than as a reference to his actual death on the cross, as H. Schürmann has carefully demonstrated.[59] Nevertheless, the language is reminiscent of the words of Jesus at the Last Supper, and this fairly clear allusion can throw light on the earlier part of the discourse of Jesus and suggest that the thought of Jesus as the bread of life is linked in some way to the metaphor used at the Last Supper when he said that the bread represented his body, *i.e.* himself. The question which interrupts the discourse leads on to a fuller exposition of these points. The Jews ask, 'How can this man give us his flesh to eat?' The question is not

answered directly. Instead Jesus reaffirms his earlier remarks all
the more strongly by stating that those who want life must both
eat his flesh and drink his blood. The person who does this will
be brought into a close union with Jesus, expressed in terms of
mutual indwelling.

The inclusion of the blood in the statement of Jesus alongside
his flesh is inescapably reminiscent of the Lord's Supper. The
passage could then be understood as referring primarily to the
sacrament and suggesting that the way to partake of the flesh
and blood of Jesus is by eating the bread and drinking the cup.
But it is most unlikely that this is the meaning of the passage.
First, there is no reference here to eating bread and drinking
wine or the cup. Jesus is not explaining that one can partake of
him by partaking of the elements in the Lord's Supper. Rather
the language of the Lord's Supper is being used metaphorically
to bring out all the more clearly the sacrificial nature of the
death of Jesus. Alongside the reference to the flesh of Jesus
we have a reference to his blood which indicates unmistakably
the sacrificial significance of his death. Second, since Jesus has
already spoken of giving his flesh for the life of the world, the
reference here would appear to be the same, and since he has
already spoken of eating as being tantamount to believing, the
point here is to underline the importance of believing in him as
the sacrifice for the life of the world. Third, in v. 63 Jesus
emphasises that 'it is the spirit that gives life, the flesh is of no
avail; the words that I have spoken to you are spirit and life.' It
is nothing fleshly which gives life, not even the physical body of
Jesus, except as it is given in death. A number of commentators
think that there is a definite reference to the 'eucharistic' flesh
of Jesus, *i.e.* to the bread, so that Jesus is denying that the bread
of the Lord's Supper can give life. It is the words of Jesus that
convey life as they are accepted and believed. That is to say, if
there is an allusion to the sacrament here, the point is that the
material symbols and the outward rite do not convey life. They
can serve as an outward symbol of spiritual participation, but
they are not the means of it. What matters is faith in Jesus, and
if the sacrament can help belief, well and good. But faith is not
tied to the sacrament. It is spoken of here both as an once-for-
all act in v. 53 and as a continuing action in vs. 54–58 in a way
which is hardly consistent with limiting the thought to sacramental experiences.[60]

Our exposition of John 6 has shown that the language of the
Lord's Supper provides one of the metaphorical expressions

through which Jesus elucidates the meaning of faith in himself as the crucified source of life. The concept of Jesus as the giver of 'real' bread is powerfully developed in a way that shows that this function is not limited to the Lord's Supper in any kind of way. The eternal life of which Jesus speaks is a constant relation of communion with the Father and the Son, and is not a fitful experience tied to specific sacramental occasions.

It is doubtful whether we should see eucharistic motifs elsewhere in John. There is nothing in the story of the miracle at Cana, where Jesus turned water into wine, to suggest that the motif of wine is being developed in a eucharistic manner.[61] Nor should we see eucharistic significance in the imagery of the vine in John 15, since there is no allusion whatever to the wine in this context and the significance of the vine is developed in quite a different direction. It is true that Jesus spoke at the Last Supper of 'the fruit of the vine', but nothing suggests that this phrase lies behind the development of vine-imagery of John 15; the sources lie rather in the OT use of the vine as a symbol of Israel and perhaps in the golden vine of Herod's temple.[62] Finally, it is very dubious that we should see any eucharistic imagery in John 19:34 with its reference to the blood and water that flowed from the side of Jesus.[63]

We should not attach too much significance to the silence of John regarding the Last Supper. One is tempted to say that it is perhaps only those who expect to find eucharistic language in every nook and cranny of the New Testament who will find the absence of it in John at all strange and draw the conclusion that its very absence constitutes a negative attitude towards it.

Nevertheless, our investigation suggests that in this Gospel we do have a critical attitude which has probably been activated by misunderstanding and misuse of the sacrament in the church. The tendency which we saw in Corinth towards regarding the Lord's Supper as a guarantee against apostasy and the definite tendency in the second century towards interpreting the elements as 'the medicine of immortality'[64] may well have been showing themselves in the Johannine church. John's fairly consistent polemic against a faith that bases itself on merely outward considerations would support this hypothesis and suggest that he found it necessary to play down the importance of a sacrament which was liable to misunderstanding and misuse, and to emphasise that its function is to spell out in visible form the need for a spiritual response to Jesus. It is the Spirit, working through the words of the crucified and glorified Jesus, who prompts faith and bestows eternal life, and this life is a spiritual communion with the Father and the Son. Therefore, John has presented an equivalent to the words of institution in the context of a discourse which is concerned with the life-giving power of Jesus himself as the true bread and with the need to come to him and to believe in him. This has enabled John to omit the words of institution in the account of the Last Supper and to develop the teaching of Jesus on that occasion, so that again it is the words which he speaks, which are spirit and life, which occupy the centre of the stage.

To describe such an attitude as anti-sacramental is false. To describe it as critically-sacramental would be nearer the mark. But it may be more satisfactory to say that John's attitude is governed by a heightened sacramental interest, if we may use the word 'sacramental' in the somewhat broader sense that John presents teaching by Jesus in which various ordinary objects, bread, water, light are seen as symbols for spiritual realities.[65]

Within the Johannine literature there is one other text that should be briefly mentioned.[66] In Revelation 3:20 we have the promise of the risen Lord: 'Behold, I stand at the door and knock; if any one hears my voice and opens the door, I will come in to him and eat with him, and he with me.' This saying is addressed to the individual members of a church which stood in danger of divine judgment and is a promise of reward to those who repent of their sin and are prepared to welcome Jesus. Although it is not primarily an evangelistic appeal to the outsider, but is directed more to the backslider, it has undoubtedly an application as wide as the universality of the gospel offer of salvation (*cf.* Rev. 22:17). The reward is expressed in terms of a meal shared by Jesus and the faithful disciple. Nothing is said about the nature of the food, and the idea of feeding on Jesus is absent. Rather the picture is one of the close fellowship of the meal table. Jesus offers to the individual believer a communion with him such as ought to be experienced in the Lord's Supper when he is present as the guest who becomes the host (Luke 24:29f.). Alternatively, the imagery may be rather that of the heavenly banquet at which Jesus is the host and the faithful are his guests. The individualisation of the promise strongly suggests that the reference is not directly to the heavenly banquet; the use of the phrase 'I will come in to him' also militates against this view. Rather, we have an anticipation of the heavenly banquet in the spiritual communion of the believer with Jesus.[67] Although, then, the imagery may be drawn from the heavenly banquet rather than the Lord's Supper, it is hard not to see here an indication of what the Lord's Supper is meant to be, namely an occasion for spiritual fellowship between the Lord and his guests, as they share a common meal.

IS THE LORD'S SUPPER MENTIONED IN THE EPISTLE TO THE HEBREWS?

One final area of New Testament teaching demands brief consideration as we come to the end of this survey of the place and significance of the Lord's Supper in the early church. The Epistle to the Hebrews presents us with a problem comparable with that which we have observed in the Gospel of John. Does the Lord's Supper have any place in this epistle? Possible allusions to it have been traced in some half-a-dozen passages, but while some of them may contain language that reflects the eucharistic usage of the early church,[68] there is only one place where there is possibly a direct allusion to the celebration of the Lord's Supper. In Hebrews 13:10 the writer comments, 'We have an altar from which those who serve the tent have no right to eat.' This verse is far from easy to understand, but three explanations of it have been offered.

The first is that the reference is to the sacrifice of Christ as pledged to believers in the Lord's Supper. The table of the Lord is then the Christian altar at which believers can, as it were, eat the sin-offering, while the Jewish priests could never do so.[69] This explanation is unlikely for two reasons. First, what the author is saying is that the Christian altar is one on which a sacrifice is offered which cannot be eaten by the worshippers because it is a sin-offering; the animals in question were slain away from the altar and burnt, and only their blood was offered on the altar. Second, it is extremely unlikely that the Author of Hebrews would have envisaged the Jewish altar being replaced by a material, Christian one. This is particularly obvious from the fact that he goes on to speak of spiritual sacrifices being offered by Christians.

The second possibility is that the Author thinks of Calvary as the Christian altar.[70] In this case it would be possible to interpret the Lord's Supper as the post-sacrificial meal, in the same way as in 1 Corinthians 10:18–22.[71] This view is open to the same objection as the first, namely that the Author is thinking of a sacrifice which was not followed by a post-sacrificial meal.

The third view is that the Author is thinking of a heavenly

altar on which the blood of Jesus, who had 'suffered outside the gate', was offered to God as an atonement for the sins of the people.[72] This seems to be much the most probable understanding of the passage. If so, it is possible to claim that the Author is denying that there is any kind of materialistic participation in sacrificial food as the Lord's Supper.[73] Alternatively, there may be no reference, polemically or otherwise, to the Lord's Supper at all.[74] This second suggestion is probably to be preferred. The Author is insisting that there is no sacrifice in the Christian church. He certainly would not have considered the Lord's Supper as a sacrifice, whether or not he is concerned deliberately to exclude the thought here. Instead, he insists that the only sacrifices which can be offered by Christians are those of lips which praise God, and of lives used in the service of others (Heb. 13:15f.). This evidence certainly does not compel us to join those scholars who insist that the Lord's Supper was not celebrated in the Author's church or that he disapproved of it.

CHAPTER SIX

Conclusion

Our investigation of the Last Supper and the Lord's Supper has embraced a number of fields of study. We began by discussing the background of the last meal held by Jesus, and looked at possible influences in the life of Judaism. Second, we made a literary investigation of the texts describing the Last Supper in order to come as near as possible to the original form of the account of this meal. Third, we asked the historical question as to what kind of meal Jesus held and what he did at it, and also as to how the early church celebrated the Lord's Supper. Fourth, there was the theological question regarding the significance of the actions of Jesus and of the early church. In this concluding section we shall endeavour to sum up and draw together the results of our discussion and to suggest very briefly the practical implications that this may have for the church today.

THE NATURE OF THE LAST SUPPER

We observed that in the synoptic Gospels the last meal of Jesus with his disciples is presented as a Passover meal. This understanding of the meal was confirmed by various features in the narrative which appear to be integral to it and not simply removable pieces of scenery placed in position on the stage by the Evangelists or their predecessors. We considered the various objections which have been lodged on historical grounds against this understanding of the meal, and concluded that they were lacking in force. The one point that was really significant was the dating of the meal a day early in the Gospel of John. Various ways of explaining this difference were considered, and we claimed that there was most to be said for the view that Jesus followed a Pharisaic calendar which was one day ahead of the official Sadducean calendar. This view requires either that it was possible to slaughter the Passover lambs a day earlier than the official festival or that those who celebrated the meal early did so without a lamb; the Gospels assume that Jesus and his disciples had a lamb for the meal, although Jesus made no reference to it in his new interpretation of the symbolism of the food; hence the former of these possibilities is more likely.

If this view is correct, we can ignore other influences, such as that of the Qumran communal meal, on the form of the Last Supper, although the fact that Jewish groups held common meals can have influenced the general practice of eating together by Jesus and his disciples.

The historicity of the meal itself is doubted by nobody, but it is sometimes doubted whether we have a reliable record of what happened at it. The debate has centred on the central feature of the meal, the so-called eucharistic actions and sayings of Jesus. We examined the texts which contain the narrative of this event, and we showed that they contain various elements in common which belong to the earliest traceable form of the tradition. Although we argued that on the whole the case for regarding the Lucan/Pauline form of the tradition as being more primitive in detail is the stronger, we recognised that this conclusion is not free from difficulty and that we must be content to accept some uncertainty regarding the precise original wording of the tradition. The question then arises whether this tradition rests on history. We argued for the early date of the tradition, as attested by Paul, and for its initial preservation and transmission in an account of the passion of Jesus, and we further claimed that the record of what Jesus did and said at the Last Supper coheres with what we know of his earlier ministry. While the actions and words of Jesus are intelligible in terms of an Old Testament and Jewish background, they contain sufficient novel features to allow us to invoke the so-called 'criterion of dissimilarity' in favour of their authenticity. It is not possible to defend the historicity of Jesus' actions and sayings by arguing for their dissimilarity from those of the early church since the express purpose of the Lord's Supper was to repeat what Jesus had done in memory of him, but we can argue that the church's practice finds its best explanation on the assumption that it was following the example and precept of Jesus. That is to say, there are no reasonable historical objections to the historicity of the Last Supper narrative, and there is good evidence in support of its historicity.

To say this in broad terms is one thing; to claim that the tradition of the words of institution is historical in every detail is another. Many scholars would attempt to draw some kind of scheme of development from a simple form of meal held by Jesus with little or even no verbal interpretation to the more developed sayings of interpretation which appear in varied forms in the later reports of the meal. But, although it is clear that a certain amount of evolution took place and resulted in the slightly differing reports which we have in the Gospels and in Paul, we have not found it necessary to assume the kind of development in which the content of the sayings of interpretation is largely attributed to the church rather than to Jesus. We have seen that as far back as we can trace it the church's meal included the ritual of the Lord's Supper. There was certainly development in the form of the meal, and it was possible for changes in understanding to take place in certain circles which led to corrective teaching by some of the New Testament writers. But these factors do not affect the point at issue, which is that we have no evidence that the original last meal of Jesus with his disciples was substantially different from the Last Supper as reported in the Gospels.

We are, then, to envisage the Last Supper as a Passover meal which would have a religious character from the start, reminding those who shared in it that they were part of the people of God who had been brought out of Egypt by his mighty action, who had been joined to him by the covenant in the wilderness, and who could look forward to the mighty hand of God bringing salvation to his people in the future. For Jesus this particular meal was the last one which he would share with his disciples before they shared in the heavenly feast in the kingdom of God. It was a farewell meal, attended by all the solemnity of such an occasion. But Jesus took the Passover meal and proceeded to give a new significance to it as a meal whose repetition by his followers would enable them to remember him. Instead of reinterpreting the Passover lamb – a step which was later taken in the early church – he used the bread and cup as symbols. In a context of redemption by sacrifice he spoke of his own death as a sacrifice inaugurating a new covenant; the bread was to represent his body given in death for the people, and the cup was to represent his blood shed in sacrifice and so establishing the new covenant. Those who partook of the bread and cup thus formed a fellowship through their common participation in the benefits brought about by his sacrificial offering of himself.

THE 'PRACTICE' OF THE LORD'S SUPPER

Following the intention of Jesus, whether implicit or as expressed in the command to repeat the action, the early church met together for fellowship meals which included this rite, known as the Breaking of Bread. In all probability these meals represented a continuation of the meals which the disciples, or rather the inner circle of them, had enjoyed with one another and with Jesus during his ministry. Since Jesus had appeared to them at mealtimes after his resurrection, the early Christians regarded their continuing meals together as occasions when Jesus himself was still present with them, though now unseen. At first such meals were held daily, and we do not know for certain whether the Breaking of Bread formed a part of the meal each time it was held or was celebrated less frequently. Nor do we know how long the church continued to meet daily in this way. Certainly by the time that 1 Corinthians was written we gain the impression that the Breaking of Bread was an integral part of the meal and that the meal was held on Sundays; the same impression can be drawn from Acts 20:7–11 which describes a scene roughly contemporary with that pictured in 1 Corinthians. There may have been a special feast associated with the annual Passover season in memory of the death and resurrection of Jesus.

The Christian meals no doubt took differing forms from place to place and from time to time. Any attempt to provide a composite picture on the basis of the different pieces of evidence must consequently be resisted, but we can draw together the various items that were associated with the meal at one time or another. It is clear that such occasions normally included Christian instruction, together with prayers and the singing of hymns. There is some debate as to whether the Christians met for instruction and praise of this kind apart from their meetings to celebrate the Lord's Supper, but on the whole it is more probable that they did; the description of a Christian meeting in 1 Corinthians 14 gives the impression that it was a separate occasion from the church meal described earlier in the same letter.[1] But there is no doubt that teaching was an integral part of the church meal. The extended teaching that followed the meal in Luke 22 and John 14–16 points in this direction. The endings of some of the Pauline letters and of the Revelation may have been phrased so as to lead on to the celebration of the Lord's Supper.

The precise relationship of the teaching, the church meal and the actual Breaking of Bread is not clear and can well have varied. The formula preserved in 1 Corinthians 11:23–25 has been thought to testify to a time when the distribution of the bread and the sharing of the cup were separated from each other by the 'supper', but this may be nothing more than a description of what happened at the Last Supper. In any case, the bringing together of the two actions in the formula and the movement of phrases between the bread-saying and cup-saying indicates that the two actions were linked together at an early stage. By the second century the Breaking of Bread or Lord's Supper had been completely separated from the church meal, but they belonged together in New Testament times. It seems most likely that the order in Corinth was teaching, the Breaking of Bread, and the common meal, with the proviso that some members of the church were indulging their hunger and thirst before the start of the proceedings.

If we may regard the closing verses of 1 Corinthians as a lead-in to the Lord's Supper, we can draw the conclusion that the Supper was introduced by the kiss of peace as a sign of loving fellowship among the members. This was accompanied both by the pronouncement of a curse upon any who did not truly love the Lord and by the pronouncement of a blessing upon the Lord's people.

Thereafter we may presume that the church followed the pattern laid down in the formula of institution. Somebody appointed for the purpose took a loaf of bread, gave thanks to God for it, presumably in a free prayer that was concerned with the Lord's gift of food both material and spiritual, then broke it in pieces and distributed it to the congregation with the words that Jesus had first used at the Last Supper. The same ritual was then followed with the common cup of wine. There is some evidence that wine may not always have been available, in which case the ritual was celebrated purely with bread; it should, however, be emphasised that the use of both elements was evidently the norm, since Paul always mentions both elements and since the major features of the interpretation were associated with the cup saying.

This is all that we are told about the 'practice' of the Lord's Supper in the New Testament. Readers of L. Goppelt's outstanding history of *Apostolic and Post-Apostolic Times* will be aware that he offers a somewhat fuller picture based on the framework of the Lord's Supper celebration found in Justin in the middle of the second century.[2] Valuable though this presentation is, it must be emphasised that it is basically a second-century picture, and great caution should be exercised in reading back from it the practice of the church a full century earlier. In any case, if we are attempting to use the practice of the early church as a norm for current practice at the Lord's Supper, it is the pattern presented in the New Testament which must be decisive and not any hypothetical reconstruction based on later, extra-biblical sources.

THE SIGNIFICANCE OF THE LORD'S SUPPER

We must now try to draw together the various aspects of the meaning of the Lord's Supper which we find in the New Testament, once again emphasising that there must have been variety in significance and emphasis at different places and times. There is indeed such a rich catalogue of theological motifs in the Lord's Supper that it is far from easy to arrange them in a systematic manner. In his important study of *Eucharist and Eschatology* G. Wainwright has commented that older books on eucharistic theology deal with the subject under three main aspects: the presence of Christ in or at the sacrament; the relation between the cross and the sacrificial nature of the sacrament; and the fruits of communion for the individual recipient. Wainwright himself is concerned with an element that he believes has been grossly neglected in the past and needs to be restored to prominence in modern discussions, namely the eschatological nature of the sacrament; he therefore organises his discussion around three basic images which give the sacrament its eschatological dimension, namely, the messianic feast; the advent of Christ; and the first fruits of the kingdom.[3] For our part we shall follow a somewhat looser pattern.

(1). *The Old Testament background*

The categories employed for the explication of the meaning of the Lord's Supper are drawn from the Scriptures.[4] In our study of the interpretative sayings of Jesus we saw that they were based on various Old Testament texts, in particular Exodus 24; Isaiah 53 and Jeremiah 31. These are the primary sources of the language and concepts in the words of institution, but the further imagery that is found in the broader context of the Supper is likewise rooted in the Old Testament; here we may think particularly of the manna tradition found in both Paul and John.

The use of the Old Testament is not merely as a source of phraseology but is above all typological. We use this word in the sense that the Old Testament records the acts of God which are seen to have correspondences in the experience of the early church, with the important proviso that the new act transcends the old. The element of prophetic fulfilment is also present of course, but it is significant that the prophecy of Jeremiah which finds fulfilment is that of a new covenant which corresponds typologically to the Mosaic covenant.

Thus the relation of the Lord's Supper and the events to which it bears witness to the Old Testament is that it stands in the context of God's saving deeds in the past and offers a typological and prophetic fulfilment. In a certain sense the Israelites had food and drink from God in the desert; now God offers something greater to his people. Accordingly, the Lord's Supper is celebrated in an atmosphere of redemption already accomplished. It forms part of a pattern of promise and fulfilment in which the grace of God to his people is continually offered afresh.

(2). *The death of Jesus*

Even more significant than the Old Testament promises however, is the fact of the new act of redemption, the fulfilment of the promises in the death of Jesus. As the Last Supper was the farewell meal in which Jesus looked forward to his death and its saving consequences, so the Lord's Supper looks back to his death and reminds the participants of the significance of the the death. First, the words of Jesus repeated at the Supper indicate that in him the prophecy of the suffering Servant of Yahweh who pours out his soul to death and bears the sin of many is fulfilled. Second, it is probable that the death of Jesus was interpreted along the lines of the deaths of the martyrs who were regarded as dying for the people in order that the wrath of

God against the nation might come to an end. This motif is not expressly present in the Lord's Supper texts, but we saw that it most probably influenced Jesus himself, and it can be seen elsewhere in the New Testament in statements about the significance of his death.[5]

Third, the death of Jesus was probably associated with the Passover sacrifice in the context of the Lord's Supper. This conclusion can be drawn from 1 Corinthians 5:7, but it remains remarkable that it is not specifically expressed in the Lord's Supper texts themselves. We have come across only one possible allusion by Jesus to himself as the Passover lamb, and it cannot be regarded as strong evidence. Clearly, the motif was not a central one, but it was at least present in the developing theology of the early church.

Fourth, the death of Jesus is undoubtedly compared to the sacrifice which inaugurated the Mosaic covenant and is regarded as inaugurating the new covenant prophesied by Jeremiah. This means that it has a twofold significance. On the one hand, it is the token of the new fellowship inaugurated between God and his people through which the blessings of the new covenant are bestowed upon them. This sacrifice creates the church as the people of God. On the other hand, the sacrifice cleanses the human partners to the covenant from their sins and bestows forgiveness upon them.

In these various ways an interpretation of the death of Jesus as a sacrifice for sin and as the means of inaugurating the new covenant finds expression in the Lord's Supper. The function of the Lord's Supper is to proclaim the death of the Lord. That is to say, the action of the church in celebrating this meal is a proclamation of the gospel to all who are present to see and hear what is happening. The meal points to Jesus and states in the plainest terms that the centre of the gospel is the death of Jesus. Earlier we rejected the view that the Lord's Supper is meant to be a memorial to God of the death of Jesus; on the contrary the Supper is part of God's Word to man, a declaration of his willingness to forgive and to receive man.

Nothing that we have discovered in the course of our investigation has lent any weight to the idea that in any sense the sacrifice of Jesus on the cross is somehow present in the Supper, that it is re-presented to God or made contemporary. Whether or not Hebrews 13 refers to the Supper, the Author would have repudiated such a suggestion. There is certainly no indication that the participants offer anything to God; the emphasis is all on what God offers to them. No sacrifice takes place in the Lord's Supper, but the sacrifice of Jesus in dying on the cross is proclaimed to sinners. If we are to speak at all of the sacrifice of Jesus being present in the Supper, we must say that it is present in the same way, no more and no less, than it is in the preaching of the Word. For the Lord's Supper is a sacrament of the Word, a visible and tangible proclamation of the good news that Jesus died for our sins.

The Lord's Supper proclaims the universality of the offer of forgiveness through the death of Jesus. His blood is said to be poured out 'for many', a phrase which is in no sense restrictive but rather emphasises the vast totality of those for whom he died.[6] The tendency in practice has been to replace 'for many' by 'for you', so as to stress the personal nature of the offer. Both emphases are needed, and the first must not be lost as the result of a stress on the latter. The Supper proclaims that the offer of the gospel is open to all.

At the same time, the Supper goes beyond the preaching of the Word. Whereas the preaching can only be an offer, the action of the Lord's Supper includes as an indispensable element the reception of the bread and the cup by the participants. By eating the bread and drinking the cup they express their acceptance of all that is signified by the body and blood of Jesus; their eating and drinking is an outward expression of their faith in Jesus, just as in baptism their cleansing with the water is an outward expression of their willingness to be spiritually cleansed from their sins and to receive the Spirit. Thus the Lord's Supper becomes the occasion for expressing one's acceptance of Jesus and the salvation which he offers, and the fact that the Supper is a repeated occurrence indicates the continual dependence of the believer on Jesus and his continual need for forgiveness.

The result is that the Supper becomes not merely an occasion for the proclamation of the gospel and for the expression of our acceptance of it but also a means of assurance that we are truly accepted into the people of God on the basis of what Jesus has done for us. To partake in the Supper is to be one of God's people, and the fact that we can do so is a means of inspiring and confirming faith.

But does the effect of the Supper go beyond this? Is there a sense in which it is more than a means of assurance, in that it can be said actually to convey the benefits of Christ's death and passion to us in a unique way? Does our reception of the bread and cup somehow also bring us salvation? The sacrament certainly does proclaim and convey the salvation achieved by Jesus on the cross, but it does so in the same way as the preached Word. The word of the cross brings salvation to those who accept it not simply as the word of man but as the Word of God, and the saving power of the word of man is due to the Holy Spirit who is active in the proclamation (1 Thes. 1:5; 2:13). Although the Spirit is not explicitly associated with the Supper, we should probably be right in claiming that, as the Spirit works through the spoken word, so too he works through the visible proclamation of the Word in the Supper. Perhaps we may find support for this claim in John 6:63 which is broad enough in application to cover the Supper. In short, then, the Supper does convey salvation but in the same way as the preaching of the Word through the agency of the Spirit. For the Supper is the proclamation of the meaning of the death of Jesus.

(3). *The risen Lord*

Alongside this central stress on the Supper as a memorial to the death of Jesus we must now place its function as a means of fellowship with the risen Lord. Although the emphasis in Paul's words in 1 Corinthians 11:26 has sometimes led to the view that the Supper is concerned exclusively with reminding us of the death of Jesus, there is plenty of evidence to show that in the early church it was regarded as the place of meeting with the risen Lord. We saw this was particularly the case in the Gospel of Luke where the Emmaus story can be summed up as showing how the risen Lord 'was known in the breaking of the bread'. We saw that it was reasonable to suppose that the same stress was continued in Acts, although it was not given explicit expression. The same stress is to be found in Paul. He regarded the bread and the cup as the means of participation in the body and blood of Jesus, that is to say as the means of sharing in the saving benefits of his death, but at the same time he spoke of the table of the Lord in a way which suggested that he regarded believers as taking part in a meal at which the Lord is host and they have fellowship with him. Although we have carefully differentiated between participation in the body and blood of Jesus and communion or fellowship with him, we must not regard these as completely separate experiences. It is a firmly established theological principle that Christ and his benefits are inseparable, so that it is a short step from participation in salvation to communion with the Saviour. We can find this same thought in John where believers eat the bread of life which is identified with Jesus himself; to eat the bread of life is in fact to believe in Jesus and this leads to the believer and Jesus entering into communion with one another. When the risen Lord invites believers to share in supper with him in Revelation 3:20, we may well see language that can be applied to the Lord's Supper. Thus the fact is established that the Lord's Supper is an occasion of fellowship with the risen Jesus.

It goes without saying that it is with his believing people that the Lord has fellowship in the Supper. Our question is whether we can say anything more precise about the nature of his presence. A long-standing tradition identifies his presence in some way with the bread and wine. The bread and wine are said to be transformed into the body and blood of Jesus – we do not need to discuss the technicalities of this view – or somehow the presence of Jesus is associated with the elements so that they actually convey him to the recipients and are not mere signs of what they signify.[7] But there appears to be nothing of this in the New Testament. Such views arise from pressing metaphors to the point at which they cease to be metaphors. In Mark the way in which the cup-saying follows the act of drinking shows that no thought of transformation is present. For Luke it is clear that the Lord is present at the Supper as Host; he is made known in the breaking of bread. In our discussion of the Emmaus story we saw that the Lord's presence was also made known in the exposition of Scripture. His presence is known in both ways, but it is the Supper which brings out more especially the fact of communion with him. For Paul the Lord again is the host at the table. To take part in the meal by eating the bread and drinking the cup is the means of participation in his body and blood, but since the distinction between body and blood is an artificial one we are not meant to think of receiving Christ in, as it were, two stages. Rather in two different ways the Lord offers to believers the benefits of his death. In Revelation the elements are not mentioned and the thought is of a meal shared by believers with the Lord. It is John's language which suggests that by eating the body and drinking the blood of Jesus we are joined in fellowship to him. But it is John who is concerned to stress that eating and drinking is to be understood spiritually. What happens at the Supper is part of the constant relationship of fellowship between the Lord and his people, and hence there is no sense in which the presence of the Lord is tied to the elements. The Lord is present at the meal as the host.

If the Lord is with his people at the Supper in the same way as he is with them at other times, there is nevertheless an important sense in which he is especially present with them on this occasion. The well-known saying 'Where two or three are gathered in my name, there am I in the midst of them' (Mt. 18:20) indicates that there is a special sense in which the Lord is with the church, even although we should want to insist on the reality of his presence with the individual. In the same way, the Supper is the particular occasion in the life of the community which celebrates the Lord's presence. The analogy has been used of a child who is conscious of the love which his father has for him and which is the constant atmosphere in the home; yet there can be occasions when the father takes the child in his arms and expresses his love for him in a special way. The love is real and constant all the time, but it needs to be given special expression from time to time in a way that would lose its value and effect if it were continual. May we not say that the communion of the believer with the Lord is a continuous experience, but that there are high points in the relationship, and that one of these is the Lord's Supper? In this way we can do justice to the fact that 'the real presence of Christ in the Lord's Supper is exactly the same as his presence in the word – nothing more, nothing less,'[8] and yet the Lord's Supper is in a special way the occasion of his presence with his people.

(4). *The heavenly banquet*

From the past and present we must now turn to the future. The fact that the Lord's Supper is orientated towards the future has emerged time and again in our investigation. We saw that Jesus held his Last Supper as his final meal with his disciples on earth before he would eat and drink with them in the kingdom of God, and that consequently the Lord's Supper is to be seen as the meal 'between the ages'. It is an anticipation of the heavenly meal which Jesus looked forward to sharing with the Twelve. Thus the Lord himself is the host who presides at the table. The church which looks forward to his coming and cries 'Maranatha' believes that he comes and is present with his people here and now. The disciples who take part are the company of the redeemed, and already they celebrate the final victory and salvation of God. They feed on heavenly food and anticipate the joys of heaven itself.

But the nature of the Supper is such that it testifies to the incompleteness of salvation. It brings out the tension between the elements of 'already' and 'not yet' in the church's hope.

Already by faith we participate in the heavenly banquet and enjoy the blessings of the age to come secured by the Saviour's death and mediated by his risen presence. But not yet are we taken out of the flesh and freed from temptation and suffering. We endure as seeing the invisible.

It is at this point that we may bring in the elements of thanksgiving and joy which mark the Lord's Supper. The heavenly meal is a scriptural picture for the enjoyment of salvation in terms of communion with the Lord. Such an experience, already vouchsafed to his people, must inevitably lead to the expression of joyfulness and praise to God. This element is expressed principally in Luke who shows how the early Christians rejoiced and praised God for their experience of salvation through the risen Lord. There is no conflict between this element and the solemnity and reverence which Paul commends as appropriate at the meal. For there is a distinction between the kind of joy which expresses itself in frivolity and which in the present context is based on a purely sensual or 'fleshly' enjoyment of the material gifts of food (*cf.* Jude 12), and the kind of joy which springs from a realisation of the goodness of God experienced in his gifts both material and spiritual. It is the element of reverence for God as the giver and provider which prevents Christian joy from degenerating into a worldly kind of pleasure. The New Testament does not appear to associate sorrow or mourning over the death of Jesus with the celebration of the Supper. The supper was not an occasion for mourning over his death, but rather for rejoicing in his presence and giving thanks for the benefits procured by his death. Whatever may have happened in a later period, the early church remembered at the Supper what the Lord's death had provided rather than grieved over the fact that he had to die. The joy of salvation experienced and the hope of its heavenly consummation were dominant.

(5). *The church's meal*

It should scarcely need saying that the Lord's Supper is the church's meal. Although the individual can enjoy fellowship with the Lord, the Supper is a feast shared by the Lord's people. This arises from the very nature of God's action in Jesus which was to inaugurate a new covenant, that is, to create a people to enjoy communion with him and to serve him. At the Supper the people are present as a people, as a church. The imagery of the one loaf is used to symbolise their unity as the body of Christ.

Thus the Supper is the focus of Christian unity. It is the

occasion for the demonstration of love among believers, expressed symbolically in the kiss of peace. There is good reason to suppose that at the Supper the concern of believers for one another was expressed tangibly. The Supper at Corinth was probably a common meal at which the believers provided for one another's needs for food and drink. The references to the Breaking of Bread in Acts 2:42–47 suggest that the sharing of goods for the benefit of the poor was associated with the meal, and it may be that we should draw the reference to 'serving tables' in Acts 6:1f. into the discussion. Such concern would fit in with the practice of the Jews at the Passover feast.

The vital importance of this element in the Supper is seen in the strong comments of Paul on those who made a mockery of it by not discerning the body and despising the church of God. To fail to show love at the Lord's Supper is to fail to realise the true nature of the Supper and hence to come under divine judgment. There were, of course, other misunderstandings of the Supper. There was a perhaps inevitable tendency to overstress the physical elements of bread and wine and to regard these as actually conveying the gift of salvation in a semi-magical manner, and so protecting participants from the dangers of apostasy and find loss of salvation. There was the failure to realise that the Supper is symbolical of an exclusive relationship with the Lord which rules out the possibility of any kind of worship of idols, and Paul speaks out strongly about the danger of judgment for those who treat their allegiance to the Lord in a light-hearted manner (1 Cor. 10:22). The placing of the question 'Is it I?' in the Last Supper narrative is clearly meant to warn believers against their own temptation to deny or betray their Lord.

(6). *The basis of theological reflection*

These five points sum up the main theological emphases of the Lord's Supper. We have seen that it stands in continuity with the acts of God in the Old Testament, that it brings out the saving significance of the Lord's death, that it is an occasion for communion with the risen Lord, that it is an anticipation of the heavenly banquet, and that it is an expression of fellowship within the body of Christ. One further point which must be briefly mentioned is that the Lord's Supper provided a major impetus for the development of Christian theology. The range of theological themes which we have discussed is broad and varied. Christian theology finds its focus in the Lord's Supper and in baptism. It was the process of meditation on the significance of the events to which the Supper bears testimony that played a large part in the development of the theological vocabulary and concepts of the early church. For example, the doctrine of redemption can be traced back to its roots in Mark 10:45 and 14:24; the concept of the new covenant came into Christian theology from the cup-saying of Jesus; and the significance of the blood of Jesus as the means of atonement probably derives from the same source. Paul's understanding of the church as the body of Christ is closely associated with the Lord's Supper. A detailed investigation would reveal how much of the language of the New Testament contains reminiscences of the sayings at the Lord's Supper. The celebration of the Lord's Supper was clearly a powerful stimulus to theological reflextion on the death of Jesus, salvation, and the church. There is a rich field here for further study.

SOME CONSIDERATIONS REGARDING THE LORD'S SUPPER TODAY

The general tone of the preceding pages has been unashamedly academic, as we have sought to establish the nature and significance of the Last Supper and the Lord's Supper in the early church. Although the exercise has been academic and exegetical, we would hope that the theological significance of the Lord's Supper for today has been apparent from time to time in the discussion. We do not intend to spell out this point any further, but rather to draw out one or two practical, almost mundane consequences from the discussion. In doing so, we are conscious of making a jump from the first century to the present day without taking into account the long history of eucharistic doctrine and practice in the intervening centuries. During this period much has been done to provide fresh ways of expressing the significant features of the Supper, although on occasion the message has been blurred and distorted. But if the church lives by Scripture and must constantly reform itself in the light of Scripture, then it may be useful to place alongside our contemporary practices some principles that appear to us to be scriptural and relevant to the modern understanding of the Lord's Supper. These will be stated briefly in thesis form.

(1). In line with what appears to have been the practice of the early church in the New Testament the Lord's Supper should be celebrated frequently in the church, and there is good reason for doing so on each Lord's Day.

(2). The New Testament links the exposition of the Scriptures and apostolic teaching with the celebration of the Lord's Supper; the Supper ought always to be an occasion for the preaching of the Word.

(3). The New Testament says nothing about who should conduct or celebrate the sacrament, and there is no evidence whatever that anything corresponding to our modern 'ordination' was essential. The celebration of the sacrament today should not be confined to those ordained to the ministry by the laying on of hands but should be open to any believer authorised by the church to do so.

(4). The New Testament says nothing about any particular conditions for participation in the sacrament beyond a willingness to come to Christ in faith and with love for other believers. The Lord's Supper today should be open to all who wish to feed on Christ and profess faith in him. This implies that unbaptised believers may take part, although it would be normal for such persons to undergo baptism without delay. It also means that there should be no barriers of age; what matters is faith and an understanding of what is happening appropriate to the age of the participant.

(5). The New Testament welcomes sinners to the Lord's table but also warns against unworthy participation in a spirit of frivolity or lovelessness. The church today in maintaining an 'open table' should also remind participants of the solemn implications of the sacrament.

(6). The Lord's Supper in the New Testament is a meal. The appropriate setting for the sacrament is a table, and the appropriate posture in our western culture is sitting. To describe the central piece of furniture as an altar is completely unjustified in terms of the New Testament understanding of the meal.

(7). The New Testament envisages the use of one loaf and a common cup. It would be good to maintain this symbolism today. Where a common cup is not practicable, the communicants may partake simultaneously. The practice whereby each person breaks a piece off a common loaf or is handed a piece broken by the celebrant or his neighbour would helpfully symbolise the breaking of the bread and the unity of the church.

(8). The New Testament does not indicate that the bread and the cup were 'consecrated' in any way for the sacrament. Neither the practice of offering the elements to God nor that of offering a prayer of epiclesis for the Spirit to bless the elements has any foundation in Scripture.

(9). In the New Testament the essential elements in the Breaking of Bread were thanksgiving and distribution of the bread and the cup in turn to the accompaniment of the interpretative sayings. In the church today we are heirs of a rich collection of prayers and other liturgical forms which elaborate on these essentially simple acts. The church today should beware lest it loses the simplicity and directness of the New Testament pattern. If, on the one hand, it is regrettable that some branches of the church fail to make use of the help and inspiration that can be drawn from the treasury of liturgy and hymnody, it is also, on the other hand, regrettable if adherence to a fixed and elaborate form of service is made the norm in other branches of the church.

(10). The New Testament celebration of the Lord's Supper included, at least on some occasions, an expression of the unity and love of believers. The inclusion of some symbol of unity appropriate to our culture, such as shaking hands, and of some expression of concern for the needy, such as the giving of money for charitable purposes, is desirable today.

(11). The New Testament itself recognises the difficulties that arose when the Lord's Supper was part of a common church meal. Nevertheless, the linking of the Supper with a meal may offer a form of fellowship that could contribute to the edification of the church today.

(12). The New Testament links together past, present and future in the significance of the Lord's Supper; it looks back to the death of Jesus for our salvation, it rejoices in the gift of present salvation and fellowship with the risen Lord, and it looks forward to his coming and the inauguration of the heavenly banquet. The church today needs to ask whether it does justice to all these elements and thus celebrates the Supper with real thanksgiving and fulness of joy.

Notes

CHAPTER ONE (pages 13–29)

1. F. Horst, TDNT V, 552.
2. Although some modern scholars doubt the authenticity of both of these commands as sayings of Jesus, the point is that the New Testament authors clearly regarded them as such and therefore as particularly authoritative.
3. Not all of these references need refer to the Lord's Supper; Acts 27:35 probably does not do so. See also Did. 14:1; Ign. Eph. 20:2.
4. The use of the term *agapē* to refer to a Christian fellowship meal should be noted (Jude 12; *cf.* 2 Pet. 2:13 *v. 1*). See below, 110f.
5. Before the legislation about the one central sanctuary came into effect sacrificial meals could take place in other localities, *e.g.* 1 Sa. 9:11–14, 22–4. See G. Delling, 'Abendmahl II. Urchristliches Mahl-Verständnis', TRE I, 47–58, especially 48.
6. H. H. Rowley, *Worship in Ancient Israel*, London, 1967, 125.
7. See A. V. Ström, 'Abendmahl I. Das sakrale Mahl in den Religionen der Welt', TRE I, 43–7, especially 45.
8. B. Klappert, 'Lord's Supper', NIDNTT II, 520–38, especially 521f.; H. Schürmann, *Der Paschamahlbericht Lk 22, (7–14.) 15–18*, München, 1953, 61f.
9. B. Klappert, NIDNTT II, 522. For a full description of a Jewish formal meal see SB IV:2, 611–39.
10. J. Jeremias, *Jerusalem in the Time of Jesus*, London, 1969, 246–52; S. Westerholm, *Jesus and Scribal Authority*, Lund, 1978, 13–15. For the view that these groups provide the model for the Last Supper see H. Lietzmann, *Mass and Lord's Supper*, Leiden, 1979, 165–71, 185.
11. See J. Jeremias, *The Eucharistic Words of Jesus*, London, 1966, 29–31.
12. G. H. Box, 'The Jewish Antecedents of the Eucharist', JTS 3, 1901–02, 357–69.
13. W. O. E. Oesterley, *The Jewish Background of the Christian Liturgy*,

Oxford, 1925, 167–79. For a similar view see K. Bornhäuser, *The Death and Resurrection of Jesus Christ*, Bangalore, 1958, 74–6. For criticism see J. Jeremias, *op. cit.*, 26–9.

14. J. B. Segal, *The Hebrew Passover from the Earliest Times to A.D. 70*, London, 1963; H. Haag, *Vom alten zum neuen Pascha*, Stuttgart, 1971.

15. J. Jeremias, *op. cit.*, 84–8; *id.*, TDNT V, 896–904; G. J. Bahr, 'The Seder of Passover and the Eucharistic Words', Nov. T. 12, 1970, 181–202; B. Schaller, 'Feast', NIDNTT I, 632–4. See Table 1.

16. G. J. Bahr, *op. cit.*, 189, claims that the guests each said their own grace.

17. J. Jeremias, *The Eucharistic Words of Jesus*, 85f. However, G. J. Bahr, *op. cit.*, 196, argues that the *haggadah* was said while the main course was being eaten. He claims that the unusual practices which prompted the son's questions did not take place until the meal was being eaten, and that it is unlikely that the food was allowed to get cold while the questioning and answering went on. However, the *haggadah* was followed by the singing of the *hallel* and it is less easy to imagine this taking place while the guests were eating.

18. Pesahim 10:4–5, cited from H. Danby, *The Mishnah*, Oxford, 1933, 150f.

19. Jos. Bel. 2:131f., cited from the Loeb translation by H. St. J. Thackeray, vol. II, Cambridge, Mass., 1927.

20. 1QS 6:3–5, cited from A. Dupont-Sommer, *The Essene Writings from Qumran*, Oxford, 1961.

21. M. Black, *The Scrolls and Christian Origins*, London, 1961, 102–15.

22. B. Gärtner, *The Temple and the Community in Qumran and the New Testament*, Cambridge, 1965, 3 n. 4.

23. 1Q28a 2:11–22.

24. The point of the last sentence of the passage would seem to be that the same procedure is to be followed at ordinary meals of the sect, the only difference being the absence of the Messiah.

25. M. Black, *op. cit.*, 109–11.

26. See further K. G. Kuhn, 'The Lord's Supper and the Communal Meal at Qumran', in K. Stendahl (ed.), *The Scrolls and the New Testament*, London, 1958, 65–93; and the critical comments by J. Jeremias, *The Eucharistic Words of Jesus*, 31–6; H. Patsch, *Abendmahl und historischer Jesus*, Stuttgart, 1971, 28–34; H. Braun, *Qumran und das Neue Testament*, Tübingen, 1966, II, 29–44.

27. M. Philonenko, *Joseph et Aseneth*, Leiden, 1968, gives the text and a commentary. For its possible significance for our study see G. D. Kilpatrick, 'The Last Supper', Exp.T 64, 1952–3, 4–8.

28. *Joseph and Asenath* 8:5, cited from the translation by E. W. Brooks, London, 1918. I have modernised the English.

29. *Ibid.*, 16:15f.

30. W. Nauck, *Die Tradition und der Charakter des ersten Johannesbriefes*, Tübingen, 1957, 147–82. *Cf.* T. W. Manson, 'Entry into Membership of the Early Church', JTS 48, 1947, 25–33.

31. K. G. Kuhn, *op. cit.*

32. M. Black, *op. cit.*, 105f.; J. Jeremias, *op. cit.*, 33f.; H. Patsch, *op. cit.*, 26–8; H. Schürmann, *Jesu ureigener Tod*, Freiburg, 1976, 76.
A further attempt to find a Jewish background to the Lord's Supper is offered by W. von Meding, '1 Korinther 11,26: Vom geschichtlichen Grund des Abendmahls', Ev.T 35, 1975, 544–52. He finds a background

in the practice attested in Jer. 16:7 of comforting mourners with bread
and a cup. But there is no trace of this motif in the texts; they reflect a
farewell meal *before* the death of Jesus and contain no element of mourning over his death.

33. A. D. Nock, *Early Gentile Christianity and its Hellenistic Background*,
    New York, 1964, 72–6.
34. H. Lietzmann, *Mass and Lord's Supper*, 182.
35. J. Jeremias, *op. cit.*, 238–43.
36. S. Neill, *The Interpretation of the New Testament 1861–1961*, London,
    1964, 171.
37. L. Goppelt, TDNT VIII, 213f.
38. See especially S. Aalen, 'Das Abendmahl als Opfermahl im Neuen
    Testament', Nov.T 6, 1963, 128–52.
39. H. Patsch, *op. cit.*, 18–23. He comments: 'Eichhorn's verdict still stands
    seventy years later: "We cannot confirm the existence of such a sacra-
    mental meal that would have provided a model for the Lord's Supper."'
    Cf. G. Delling, TRE I, 48.

CHAPTER TWO (pages 30–56)

1. H. Braun, *Jesus*, Stuttgart, 1969, 50.
2. R. Bultmann, *Theology of the New Testament*, London, 1952, I, 144–51;
   id., *The History of the Synoptic Tradition*, Oxford, 1968², 265f. Bultmann
   traces his view back to A. Eichhorn and W. Heitmüller at the turn of
   the century. For similar views see W. Marxsen, *The Lord's Supper as a
   Christological Problem*, Philadelphia, 1970, and the writers cited in R.
   Pesch, *Das Abendmahl und Jesu Todesverständnis*, Freiburg, 1978, 9–21.
   A number of scholars who accept that Jesus held a last meal with his
   disciples hold that the words of institution of the Lord's Supper may
   nevertheless be a creation by the church; see E. Schweizer, *The Lord's
   Supper according to the New Testament*, Philadelphia, 1967, 26.
3. J. Jeremias, *The Eucharistic Words of Jesus*. Similar views are adopted by
   such scholars as A. J. B. Higgins, *The Lord's Supper in the New Testament*,
   London, 1952; W. Barclay, *The Lord's Supper*, London, 1967; H.
   Schürmann, *Jesu ureigener Tod*; L. Goppelt, *Theologie des Neuen Testaments*, Göttingen, 1975, I, 261–70; H. Patsch, *Abendmahl und historischer
   Jesus*. R. Pesch, *op. cit.*
4. K. Wegenast, NIDNTT III, 772–5. The analogy with Jewish tradition
   has been questioned by C. K. Barrett, *The First Epistle to the Corinthians*,
   London, 1968, 264f., since the same vocabulary is found in Greek usage.
5. H. Schürmann, *Der Einsetzungsbericht Lk 22, 19–20*, Münster, 1955,
   7–14; *cf.* J. Jeremias, *op. cit.*, 103–05; P. Neuenzeit, *Das Herrenmahl:
   Studien zur paulinischen Eucharistieauffassung*, München, 1960, 86.
6. The date is established by an inscription which fixes the governorship of
   Gallio (Acts 18:12–17) in AD 51–52 (or AD 52–53). See, for example,
   R. Jewett, *Dating Paul's Life*, London, 1979, 38–40.
7. C. K. Barrett, *op. cit.*, 265f. J. Jeremias, *op. cit.*, 202f., observes that the
   word 'from' (*apo*) signifies that the eucharistic words cited by Paul from
   the tradition go back to Jesus himself. However, G. Bornkamm, *Early*

Christian Experience, London, 1969, 130f., thinks that the 'Lord' is the heavenly Lord who speaks in the tradition.
8. J. Jeremias, *op. cit.,* 185f.; P. Neuenzeit, *op. cit.,* 86.
9. See above, 27–9.
10. R. Pesch, *op. cit.,* 54f. Cf. L. Goppelt, *op. cit.,* I, 261, who holds that Paul received the formula shortly after his conversion in Damascus.
11. H. Schürmann, *Der Einsetzungsbericht,* 2–7; R. Pesch, *op. cit.,* 24f.; D. P. Senior, *The Passion Narrative according to Matthew,* Leuven, 1975, 76–88. The point appears to be uncontested. It is true that some recent scholars defend the general priority of Matthew over against Mark, but to the best of my knowledge none of them has examined this particular passage in detail in order to demonstrate that Matthew was here the source for Mark. The only dispute concerns whether the changes in Matthew's version reflect liturgical usage (H. Patsch, *op. cit.,* 69f.) or editing by Matthew (see the scholars cited above). Probably both factors were at work. See below, 99–101.
12. An echo of this saying of Jesus is probably to be found in Paul's addition 'until he comes' which catches the eschatological note present in it.
13. R. Bultmann, *The History of the Synoptic Tradition,* 265; V. Taylor, *The Gospel according to St. Mark,* London, 1953, 542f.
14. The statement in the text assumes the originality of the 'longer' text of Luke 22:19f. See below, 36–8, for the question whether this form of the text is original.
15. H. Schürmann, *Der Paschamahlbericht,* argues that the eucharistic narrative (Lk. 22:19f.) was composed as an appendix to this 'Passover' narrative to clarify what was obscure in it. See below, 55f.
16. R. Bultmann, *ibid.*
17. I. H. Marshall, *The Gospel of Luke,* Exeter, 1977, 792–4.
18. R. Pesch, *op. cit.,* 70f. (Pesch's monograph discusses at greater length many of the points raised in his commentary, *Das Markusevangelium,* II. Teil, Freiburg, 1977, here 354, 356; we shall give references to the commentary only where the matter is not contained in the monograph).
19. H. Patsch, *op. cit.,* 95–102.
20. Representatives of this view include: J. Behm, TDNT III, 730–2; W. Marxsen, *The Lord's Supper as a Christological Problem,* 4–8; G. Bornkamm, *Early Christian Experience,* 134–8; E. Schweizer, *The Lord's Supper according to the New Testament,* 10–17; P. Neuenzeit, *op. cit.,* 103–120.
21. J. Jeremias, *The Eucharistic Words of Jesus,* 138–203 (but see n. 23 below); A. J. B. Higgins, *The Lord's Supper in the New Testament;* B. Klappert, NIDNTT II, 524–6; H. Patsch, *op. cit.,* 59–105; R. Pesch, *op. cit.,* 34–51.
22. H. Schürmann, *Der Einsetzungsbericht;* I. H. Marshall, *op. cit.,* 799–807 (with hesitation).
23. J. Jeremias, *op. cit.,* 189–91; H. Patsch, *op. cit.,* 87–9; G. Delling, TRE I, 48.
24. M. Rese, 'Zur Problematik von Kurz- und Langtext in Luk. XXII. 17ff.', NTS 22, 1975–76, 15–31. See further A. Vööbus, 'A New Approach to the Problem of the Shorter and Longer Text in Luke', NTS 15, 196–69, 457–63; for a fuller list of supporters of this view see I. H. Marshall, *op. cit.,* 799–801.
25. H. Schürmann, *Der Einsetzungsbericht,* 17–42, 49–63, 65–73.
26. R. Pesch, *op. cit.,* 31–4. See further below.

27. I. H. Marshall, *Luke – Historian and Theologian*, Exeter, 1979, 170–5.
28. J. Jeremias, *op. cit.*, 156–9, *cf.* 125–37.
29. H. Schürmann, *Traditionsgeschichtliche Untersuchungen*, Düsseldorf, 1968, 159–92, especially 185–90 (originally as 'Lk. 22, 19b–20 als ursprüngliche Textüberlieferung', Bib. 32, 1951, 366–92, 522–41).
30. G. Delling, TRE I, 47–58, especially 50f., holds that the sheer variety of the attempts to deal with this question supports this view.
31. J. Ernst, *Das Evangelium nach Lukas*, Regensburg, 1977, 583f. For the evidence see J. Jeremias, *op. cit.*, 145–52.
32. The fullest treatments of the argument for the longer text are in J. Jeremias, *op. cit.*, and H. Schürmann, *op. cit.* There is an excellent summary of the whole matter in B. M. Metzger, *A Textual Commentary on the Greek New Testament*, London, 1971, 173–7.
33. J. Jeremias, *op. cit.*, 196–201, has shown that both Hebrew and Aramaic features can be seen in the wording. R. Pesch, *op. cit.*, 51–3, has re-examined the evidence and strengthened the case for a Hebrew form of the narrative. See also M. Black, *An Aramaic Approach to the Gospels and Acts*, Oxford, 1954², 268f.
34. J. Jeremias, *op. cit.*, 173–86.
35. R. Pesch, *op. cit.*, 26–34. Attention should be drawn to the curious statement by B. Klappert, NIDNTT II, 523. Having argued that 'The text of Lk ... betrays the influence ... of a text very closely related to, but older than, that of 1 Cor. 11:23–25', he concludes illogically 'So we are left with Mk. 14:22–25 and 1 Cor. 11:23–25 as the oldest forms of the tradition.'
36. H. Schürmann, *Der Paschamahlbericht Lk 22*, (*7–14.*) *15–18*; *id.*, *Der Einsetzungsbericht Lk 22, 19–20; id.*, *Jesu Abschiedsrede Lk 22, 21–38*, Münster, 1957. See also V. Taylor, *The Passion Narrative of St Luke*, Cambridge, 1972, 47–58. For Schürmann's 'retraction' see J. Jeremias, *op. cit.*, 190.
37. H. Schürmann, *Der Einsetzungsbericht*, 17–42. Pesch does not make any attempt to answer Schürmann's points in detail.
38. J. Jeremias, *op. cit.*, 154f.
39. See n. 18 above.
40. H. Schürmann, *op. cit.*, 49–56, argues that the revision stems from Paul himself, while P. Neuenzeit, *op. cit.*, 103–05, regards it as pre-Pauline (*cf.* G. Delling, TRE I, 51; R. Pesch, *op. cit.*, 39). Neuenzeit appears to have the better of the argument.
41. Once the original story had been turned into Greek, it could have existed in more than one form of words which could easily be altered in one direction or another. It is quite possible too that the shorter form is the original, and that Mark added the words 'as they were eating' under the influence of the earlier use of the phrase in Mk. 14:18.
42. H. Schürmann, *op. cit.*, 51 n. 192, 59.
43. H. Schürmann, *op. cit.*, 59.
44. For detailed discussion see H. Schürmann, *Der Paschamahlbericht*, 53–60; *cf.* H. Patsch, 71. Schürmann claims that 'to thank' quickly took on the special meaning 'to say the eucharistic thanksgiving'.
45. J. Jeremias, *op. cit.*, 52 n. 3, 115; R. Pesch, *op. cit.*, 43–5. Against the view that the Lord's Supper was celebrated frequently with bread alone see H. Schürmann, *Der Einsetzungsbericht*, 122; *Traditionsgeschichtliche Untersuchungen*, 182–4. The abbreviation in the Lucan/Pauline account

is to avoid repetition rather than to emphasise the distribution of the bread. The piling up of interpretation in the cup-saying also suggests that the use of the cup was normal.

46. J. Jeremias, *op. cit.*, 115–22.
47. H. Schürmann, *Der Einsetzungsbericht*, 87.
48. H. Patsch, *op. cit.*, 71–3. One phrase in Mark which has no equivalent in the Lucan/Pauline account is 'and they all drank of it'. It is hard to see the purpose of this comment, whether in an original or a secondary account. It may be a way of saying that Jesus himself did not partake of the cup. More probably it may be a way of underlining the fact that Judas, the traitor, also partook.
49. It is probable that Paul's phrase should be translated as 'the cup (which is drunk) after supper', *i.e.* that it designates the cup in question as the one which was used at the end of the meal (the 'cup of blessing' of 1 Cor. 10:16); *cf.* H. Schürmann, *op. cit.*, 34f. R. Pesch, 44, concludes that on this view the Pauline wording is dependent on the Marcan tradition, but this conclusion is unnecessary. Schürmann claims that if this view is correct, the slight alteration in Luke's wording means that he has altered the sense to give: 'and Jesus' action with the cup took place, like the action with the bread, after supper'. (so I. H. Marshall, *The Gospel of Luke*, 805). But Luke's wording can equally well mean 'and Jesus action with the cup, which took place after supper, was like the action with the bread'.
50. W. Marxsen, *The Lord's Supper as a Christological Problem*, makes great play with the difference between the cup and its contents, but his view is quite untenable (H. Patsch, *op. cit.*, 53–5).
51. The problem is that in the Marcan form the word 'blood' is a predicate in the nominative case, and the phrase 'which is poured out for many' stands in apposition in the same case. In the Lucan form, however, while the phrase remains unchanged, the word 'blood' is in the dative case. *Cf.* H. Patsch, *op. cit.*, 78.
52. J. Jeremias, *op. cit.*, 165f., 219; R. Pesch, *op. cit.*, 46.
53. H. Schürmann, *op. cit.*, 48f., 113f.; G. Delling, TRE I, 51.
54. R. Pesch, *op. cit.*, 46f., argues that Paul's account is not interested in the recipients of the bread and wine, and that therefore it dropped the references to giving and taking of the bread and wine. But 1 Cor. 11:25b shows that the tradition was interested in this, and Paul's own comments indicate that he was concerned primarily with the recipients. The Pauline account is concerned with what Jesus did rather than with the disciples, but it is not unconcerned about the eating and drinking, and the whole account naturally presupposes these acts.
55. H. Schürmann, *op. cit.*, 114; H. Patsch, *op. cit.*, 73f.
56. G. Dalman, *Jesus-Jeshua*, London, 1929, 161; J. Jeremias, *op. cit.*, 170.
57. See especially H. Patsch, *op. cit.*, 84f.
58. B. Klappert, NIDNTT II, 525f.
59. J. Jeremias, *op. cit.*, 167f.
60. This argument would be strengthened if we accept the view that the meal may have been celebrated with bread only, in which case it would be unlikely that essential elements of interpretation would be dropped from the bread-saying. See, however, n. 45.
61. R. Pesch, *op. cit.*, 47.
62. H. Patsch, *op. cit.*, 76. *Cf.* J. Jeremias, *op. cit.*, 167.

63. H. Schürmann, *op. cit.*, 65–9.
64. H. Schürmann, *op. cit.*, 95–112.
65. *Ibid.*, 115–23.
66. J. Jeremias, *op. cit.*, 173–86. See above, 39.
67. It has often been asserted that the phrase 'my blood of the covenant' is impossible in Hebrew or Aramaic. On the basis of this and other considerations it has been argued that the original form of the sayings was 'This is my body. This is my blood which is shed for many' (K. G. Kuhn, in K. Stendahl (ed.), *The Scrolls and the New Testament*, 80f.; E. Lohse, *Märtyrer und Gottesknecht*, Göttingen, 1955, 122–9; B. Klappert, NIDNTT II, 524–6, 532f.). R. Bultmann, *Theology of the New Testament*, London, 1952, I, 146, adopts the even briefer form 'This is my body. This is my blood'.
    However, J. A. Emerton, 'The Aramaic underlying τὸ αἱμά μου τῆς διαθήκης in Mk. XIV.24', JTS 6, 1955, 238–40, and J. Jeremias, *op. cit.*, 193–5, have convincingly shown that the phrase is possible in a Semitic language.
    The problem arises only if we regard the Marcan form of words as the older form. It does not arise with the Lucan/Pauline wording. See further, 91.
68. This was quite possible in Greek, as is shown by the variant reading in Mt. 26:28, and it does not seem impossible in a Semitic language.
69. H. Schürmann, *op. cit.*, 118f.
70. The point is discussed by H. Schürmann, *op. cit.*, 121–3. Not all of his arguments for this crucial point are convincing. He suggests that in the Marcan tradition the phrase was transferred from its original place to the cup-saying as a result of a tendency to pile up the soteriological statements surrounding the cup. It seems more likely, however, that it was the existence of both phrases as a result of the development outlined in the text that led to the suppression of one of them.
71. Cf. R. Pesch, *op. cit.*, 92f.
72. H. Schürmann, *op. cit.*, 75–7.
73. J. Jeremias, *op. cit.*, 179–82.
74. H. Schürmann, *op. cit.*, 17–30. Schürmann argues for the originality of the Lucan form with the participle 'given' (hence objections based on the impossibility of the Pauline form in a Semitic language (J. Jeremias, *op. cit.*, 167) are baseless; see, however, G. Delling, TRE I, 51f., who argues that the Pauline wording can represent a Hebrew form of words); he also claims that the phrase 'to give one's body' is perfectly possible in Hebrew thought. P. Neuenzeit's objection (*op. cit.*, 108f.) that the Pauline text is older than the Lucan is not convincing.
75. B. Klappert, NIDNTT II, 525; cf. E. Lohse, *Märtyrer und Gottesknecht*, 125.
76. See J. Jeremias, *op. cit.*, 198–201; H. Schürmann, *op. cit.*, 119f. (n. 416); H. Patsch, *op. cit.*, 83. But see below, 86.
77. I. H. Marshall, *The Gospel of Luke*, 806. For the objections to this view see H. Schürmann, *op. cit.*, 65–9, 73–80. The arguments seem to be evenly balanced.
78. H. Schürmann, *op. cit.*, 69–73. R. Pesch, *op. cit.*, 49, however, states that Luke has deleted the second occurrence of the command from the Pauline account (although he gives no reason for this statement), and that the doubling was an original feature of the tradition.

79. H. Schürmann, *op. cit.*, 123–6.
80. H. Patsch, *op. cit.*, 142–50. See also W. G. Kümmel, *Promise and Fulfilment*, London, 1957, 64–83.
81. H. Schürmann, *op. cit.*, 30–4. It can be argued that this difference in accent is simply what we would expect between a historical narrative and a liturgical rubric (I. H. Marshall, *The Gospel of Luke*, 804). However, the point is rather that the development is what we would expect if the command was historical. It is in fact the liturgical account which uses the command in the sense of remembering Jesus rather than repeating the rite, and it is unlikely that the latter sense developed out of the former.
82. M. Goguel, 'Luke and Mark: With a Discussion of Streeter's Theory', HTR 26, 1933, 1–55, citation from 31 (cited by H. Schürmann, *ibid.*, 124). Similarly, H. Patsch, *op. cit.*, 79.
83. J. Jeremias, *op. cit.*, 237f.; see P. Benoit, 'Le récit de la Cène dans Lc. XXII, 15–20', RB 48, 1939, 357–93, citation from 386.
84. H. Schürmann, *op. cit.*, 127–9.
85. H. Patsch, *ibid.*
86. Against the view that the saying has a Hellenistic origin see J. Jeremias, *op. cit.*, 238–43; H. Schürmann, *op. cit.*, 125f.
87. H. Schürmann, *Der Paschamahlbericht*, 41.
88. R. Pesch, *op. cit.*, 26–31.
89. P. Benoit, *art cit.*; W. G. Kümmel, *Promise and Fulfilment*, London, 1957, 30–2; J. Wanke, *Beobachtungen zum Eucharistieverständnis des Lukas aufgrund der lukanischen Mahlberichte*, Leipzig, 1973.
90. J. Jeremias, *op. cit.*, 160–4, 207–18; H. Schürmann, *op. cit.*, 1–74; H. Patsch, *op. cit.*, 89–95; see also V. Taylor, *The Passion Narrative of St Luke*, Cambridge, 1972, 47–50.
91. It must be allowed that Luke can make minor transpositions of order within pericopae, but the other points remain valid.
92. See especially J. Jeremias, *op. cit.*, 161, for a list of such stylistic points. H. Patsch, *op. cit.*, 94, draws particular attention to the lack of precise parallelism between vs. 16 and 18 (already noted by Schürmann) and claims that a closer parallelism would have been expected if a new pair of sayings was being created out of the Marcan saying. It could be objected, however, that Luke's literary skill shows itself in elegant variation, and that, having modelled vs. 16 closely on Mark 14:25, he indulged in variation in framing v. 18. Against this objection, however, it must be insisted that Luke is a conservative redactor of sayings of Jesus, and that we should have expected v. 18 to be closer to Mark 14:25 if he drew it from that source.
93. The early existence of a Christian Passover is defended by H. Schürmann, 'Die Anfänge christlicher Osterfeier', *Theologische Quartalschrift* 131, 1951, 414–25 (reprinted in *Ursprung und Gestalt*, Düsseldorf, 1970, 199–206). See further J. Jeremias, *op. cit.*, 122–5; TDNT V, 901–4. The oldest evidence is 1 Cor. 5:7f., but we do not know how much earlier the celebration can be traced. In any case, Jeremias admits that a Christian Passover would provide the occasion for remembering the paschal features of the Last Supper, but does not account for the content of the narrative.
94. H. Patsch, *op. cit.*, 94.
95. J. Jeremias, *The Eucharistic Words of Jesus*, 211f. However, we must ask

whether this view depends on his special interpretation of the sayings as containing a vow of abstinence from the meal. Of greater weight may be the point (*ibid.*, 191) that Mark 14:25 fits rather loosely after v. 24, and is likely to have had some kind of introduction.

CHAPTER THREE (pages 57–75)

1. E. Schweizer, *The Lord's Supper according to the New Testament*, 29, denies the presence of paschal features in the account of the institution.
2. See above, 34f.; R. Pesch, *Das Abendmahl und Jesu Todesverständnis*, 81–3; *id.*, *Das Markusevangelium* II, 1–27.
3. For much of the material in this section we are heavily dependent on J. Jeremias, *The Eucharistic Words of Jesus*, 41–62. We have not considered it necessary to cite his evidence in detail, and our discussion is confined to assessing points on which there is some uncertainty. Detailed references will not be given within this section of his book.
4. See also Luke 22:7. Although the first day of Unleavened Bread was normally reckoned as Nisan 15, it is clear that Mark means Nisan 14 here, and there is evidence that Nisan 14 could be designated as the first day of Unleavened Bread (Jos. Bel. 5:99).
5. The suggestion is treated with reserve by R. Schnackenburg, *Das Johannesevangelium*, Freiburg, 1975, III, 23.
6. See above, 21–3.
7. Luke, to be sure, does not mention the dish, but he describes the same incident (the prophecy of the betrayal) as occurring after the words of institution. On the order of the incidents see I. H. Marshall, *The Gospel of Luke*, 807f.
8. See the description of a guest meal in SB IV:2, 611–39.
9. This view is adopted by E. Schweizer, *The Good News according to Mark*, London, 1971, 294–7.
10. R. Schnackenburg, *op. cit.*, III, 37f.; E. Schweizer, *The Lord's Supper according to the New Testament*, 31.
11. E. Schweizer, *The Good News according to Mark*, 307.
12. E. Schweizer, *The Lord's Supper according to the New Testament*, 31.
13. J. Jeremias, *op. cit.*, 62–84.
14. This view is, however, adopted by J. Jeremias, *op. cit.*, 220–5. C. K. Barrett, 'Luke XXII.15: To Eat the Passover', JTS 9, 1958, 305–07, has shown that Lk. 22:15 contains a reference to the Passover Lamb.
15. J. Jeremias, *op. cit.*, 69f. See further SB IV:1, 58–61.
16. H. Schürmann, *Der Paschamahlbericht*, 60f.; *Jesu ureigener Tod*, 76f.; G. Delling, TRE I, 49.
17. So H. Schürmann, *ibid.*
18. Although this translation does not seem to be accepted in the current English versions, it is undoubtedly correct. See C. Burchard, 'Fussnoten zum neutestamentlichen Griechisch', ZNW 61, 1970, 157f.
19. R. Pesch, *Das Markusevangelium* II, 462; *cf.* I. H. Marshall, *op. cit.*, 860.
20. The interpretation of Pesahim 8:6 is disputed, and it is quite possible that Pilate's action had nothing to do with this Jewish ruling.
21. H.W. Montefiore, 'When did Jesus die?', Exp.T 72, 1960–61, 53f.
22. There was some debate among the Jews as to how the day for offering the first fruits was to be calculated. See below, 71–3.

23. J. Jeremias, *op. cit.*, 83f., 122–5.
24. Thus there was nothing strange in Jesus going to Gethsemane, which lay within the area permitted to pilgrims during the Passover night. Again, the carrying of arms by the disciples was permissible (Shabbath 6:4). The fact that Simon of Cyrene came in 'from the field' does not mean that he had been working on the festival day, but merely that he had been in the countryside.
25. See Sanhedrin 4:1. Capital trials were forbidden on the eve of a feast since the verdict could not be delivered on the same day as the trial. This rule and the rule about not holding trials by night were flouted in the case of Jesus.
26. R. E. Brown, *The Gospel according to John*, London, 1971, II, 556.
27. For supporters of this view see the lists in J. N. Geldenhuys, *Commentary on the Gospel of Luke*, London, 1950, 650; J. Jeremias, *op. cit.*, 22 n. 3.
28. See n. 8.
29. V. Taylor, *The Gospel according to St Mark*, London, 1953, 664–7; F. F. Bruce, *New Testament History*, London, 1969, 191f.
30. See A. Jaubert, *La Date de la Cène*, Paris, 1957, 108 n. 2. One could wish for some firm evidence to establish whether groups in Palestine in the first century could hold a lambless Passover meal.
31. J. Jeremias, *op. cit.*, 19f.; 79–83; J. N. Geldenhuys, *op. cit.*, 649–70.
32. R. Bultmann, *Das Evangelium des Johannes*, Göttingen, 1959[16], 352; R. Schnackenburg, *Das Johannesevangelium* III, 16.
33. C. K. Barrett, *The Gospel according to St John*, London, 1955, 364; R. E. Brown, *op. cit.*, II, 549f.
34. For the evidence see SB II, 837–40; objections to the Johannine statement have been raised by C. K. Barrett, *op. cit.*, 444, but R. Schnackenburg, *op. cit.*, III, 278, regards them as indecisive.
35. J. N. Geldenhuys, *op. cit.*, 660–3, following T. Zahn, *Introduction to the New Testament*, Edinburgh, 1909, III, 282f., 296–8.
36. SB II, 837–40.
37. J. N. Geldenhuys, *op. cit.*, 663. As Geldenhuys states the case, it depends on the assumption that John and his readers were familiar with the synoptic Gospels in detail – an assumption which is certainly open to question.
38. L. Morris, *The Gospel according to John*, London, 1972, 778–9.
39. J. Jeremias, *op. cit.*, 80.
40. *Ibid.* The Hebrew phrase 'eve of Passover' is found in the Mishnah, but the Aramaic phrase corresponding to it is found only in late sources. *Cf.* L. Morris, *op. cit.*, 776 n. 97.
41. R. Schnackenburg, *op. cit.*, III, 306. It should be noted that if we take the phrase to mean 'Friday' this does not conflict with the view that John is depicting a crucifixion before the Passover, since all the Gospels agree that Jesus was crucified on a Friday.
42. See L. Morris, *op. cit.*, 774–86, for a frank recognition by a conservative scholar that this is the case.
43. So R. Pesch, *Das Markusevangelium* II, 324–6. He argues that a not completely successful re-working of the synoptic chronology has taken place.
44. J. Calvin, *A Harmony of the Gospels*, Edinburgh, 1972, III, 126f.
45. J. Pickl, *The Messias*, St. Louis, 1946, 120–2, as cited by H. W. Hoehner, *Chronological Aspects of the Life of Christ*, Grand Rapids, 1977, 84.
46. J. Jeremias, *op. cit.*, 24. Pickl argues that the Galileans rested on Nisan

14, and that there is evidence for an eight-day feast of Unleavened Bread. Neither of these premises for his argument seem to be well-based.

47. D. Chwolson, *Das Letzte Passamahl Christi und der Tag seines Todes*, Leipzig, 1908², 20–44, as cited by H. Hoehner, *op. cit.*, 82f.

48. J. Jeremias, *op. cit.*, 21–3.

49. SB II, 812–53, especially 847–53; *cf.* W. M. Christie, *Palestine Calling*, London, no date, 129–41.

50. J. Jeremias, *op cit.*, 23f. The other details of the theory are firmly attested. S. Dockx, *Chronologies néotestamentaires et Vie de l'Eglise primitive*, Paris/Gembloux, 1976, 21–9, argues from Mk. 14:1 that the Pharisees and Sadducees followed the same calendar; he claims that the Galileans and Judeans fixed the date of Nisan 1 and hence of the Passover independently.

51. A. Jaubert, *op. cit.*, (Eng. Tr. *The Date of the Last Supper*, New York, 1965).

52. E. Ruckstuhl, *Chronology of the Last Days of Jesus*, New York, 1965; M. Black, *The Scrolls and Christian Origins*, 199–201; *id.*, 'The Arrest and Trial of Jesus and the Date of the Last Supper', in A. J. B. Higgins (ed.), *New Testament Essays*, Manchester, 1959, 19–34.

53. J. Jeremias, *op. cit.*, 24–6.

54. M. Black, *The Scrolls and Christian Origins*, 201, argues that Jesus need not have belonged to a sectarian group to keep what many may have regarded as the 'old' calendar of Israel.

55. H. W. Hoehner, *op. cit.*, 85–90; *cf.* R. T. Beckwith, 'The Day, its Divisions and its Limits, in Biblical Thought', EQ 43, 1971, 218–27.

56. At this point the defenders of this view appear to embrace the same view as J. Pickl and thus to face the same difficulties.

CHAPTER FOUR (pages 76–106)

1. I. H. Marshall, *The Gospel of Luke*, 789–91; similarly R. Pesch, *Das Markusevangelium* II, 340–5, who strongly defends the historicity of the incident.

2. J. Jeremias, *The Eucharistic Words of Jesus*, 225f.; L. Morris, *The Apostolic Preaching of the Cross*, London, 1965³, 130–3. Of decisive significance is Pesahim 10:6: 'May we eat there of the sacrifices and of the Passover-offerings whose blood has reached with acceptance the wall of thy Altar, and let us praise thee for our redemption and for the ransoming of our soul'. The sayings is attributed to R. Akiba (early second century).

3. J. Jeremias, *ibid.*, refers to the redemptive effect of the merits of the Passover blood for the people of God in the End-time. The evidence cited, however, appears to refer not to the End-time in particular, but to the way in which the Passover sacrifices will retain their effect to the End-time.

4. J. Jeremias, *op. cit.*, 252.

5. *Ibid.*, 256–62. Psalm 118 was certainly interpreted messianically in the early church and by Jesus himself.

6. Cited from M. Black, *An Aramaic Approach to the Gospels and Acts*, Oxford, 1954², 173. The poem is found in the Targum on Ex. 12:42 or 15:18. See further J. Jeremias, *op. cit.*, 206f.; R. le Déaut, *La Nuit Pascale*, Rome, 1963.

7. The roots of the concept of a future feast for God's people can be found in Is. 25:6f.; 1 Enoch 62:14; 2 Baruch 29; see also 2 Enoch 42:3ff. (as reproduced in SB IV:2, 1138 n.) and the Rabbinic material in SB IV:2, 1146f., 1154–9. The concept took varied forms. See J. Behm, TDNT II, 34f., 691.
8. L. Goppelt, *Theologie des Neuen Testaments*, Göttingen, 1975, I, 263f.
9. If the Lord's Supper was not the direct counterpart of the Passover itself, this would help to explain why it was celebrated more frequently than the latter.
10. *Cf.* R. Pesch, *Das Abendmahl und Jesu Todesverständnis*, 80.
11. H. Patsch, *Abendmahl und historischer Jesus*, 106–230.
12. J. Jeremias, *op. cit.*, 207–18.
13. F. C. Burkitt and A. E. Brooke, 'St Luke XXII. 15, 16: What is the General Meaning?', JTS 9, 1908, 569–72.
14. The Quartodecimans were a Christian group who aroused controversy in the second century by their insistence on celebrating Easter at the time of the Jewish Passover (the night of Nisan 14–15), whatever day of the week it happened to be, whereas other Christians celebrated Easter on a Sunday. See J. Jeremias, TDNT V, 901–4, for a succinct account, based on B. Lohse, *Das Passafest der Quartadecimaner*, Gütersloh, 1953.
15. H. Patsch, *op. cit.*, 131–9.
16. H. Schürmann, 'Jesu Abendmahlsworte im Lichte seiner Abendmahlshandlung', in *Ursprung und Gestalt*, 100–7; id. 'Das Weiterleben der Sache Jesu in nachösterlichen Herrenmahl', in *Jesu ureigener Tod*, Freiburg, 1975, 66–96.
17. See above, 63.
18. See above, 19.
19. G. Dalman, *Jesus-Jeshua*, 133–7, 150–3.
20. This criterion is sometimes misused to deny the historicity of sayings or actions of Jesus which do have a parallel in Judaism. Its proper use is to confirm the historicity of sayings or actions of Jesus which stand out by their uniqueness from Judaism and yet are explicable within a Jewish context.
21. This is the element of truth in H. Schürmann's discussion of the actions of Jesus as an eschatological sign of fulfilment (*Jesu ureigene Tod*, 90–95).
22. E. Stauffer, *New Testament Theology*, London, 1955, 299 n. 548, has listed seven reasons for not interpreting 'is' in terms of identity of substance. But when he claims, 'It is not the *substantia* of the bread and the wine that are the saving signs, but the act of breaking the bread and pouring out the wine, and it is these actions which stand in correlation to the offering of the body and blood of Christ', he is going against the sense of 1 Cor. 11:25 where the cup (and not the action of pouring it out) is the saving sign; *cf.* J. Jeremias, *op. cit.*, 220f.
23. G. Dalman, *op. cit.*, 141–3.
24. J. Jeremias, *op. cit.*, 198–201, 221f.; L. Goppelt, *op. cit.*, I, 265.
25. Against H. Lietzmann, *Mass and Lord's Supper*, 180f.; J. Jeremias, *op. cit.*, 223f., see J. Behm, TDNT III, 729 n. 14. The participle 'broken' is used with reference to the body of Jesus in some late MSS of 1 Cor. 11:24.
26. H. Schürmann, *Der Einsetzungsbericht*, 18f., 107–10; H. Patsch, *op. cit.*, 83; E. Schweizer, TDNT VII, 1059.

27. R. Pesch, *Das Markusevangelium* II 357; *cf.* C. E. B. Cranfield, *The Gospel according to St Mark*, Cambridge, 1959, 426; L. Goppelt, *op. cit.*, 267.

28. R. Pesch, *Das Abendmahl und Jesu Todesverständnis*, 92f.

29. The present participle has a future sense.

30. Ex. 30:14; Lv. 22:14; *cf.* Lv. 5:7; 6:23; Ezk. 43:21.

31. Is. 53:10; 2 Macc. 7:9; 8:21; 4 Macc. 1:8, 10.

32. J. Jeremias, *op. cit.*, 220–5, citation from 223.

33. See above, 63 n. 14.

34. J. Jeremias, TDNT V, 713–17; H. Schürmann, 'Wie hat Jesus seinen Tod bestanden und verstanden?', in *Jesu ureigener Tod*, 16–65. J. Roloff, 'Anfänge der soteriologischen Deutung des Todes Jesu (Mk. X. 45 und Lk. XXII. 27)', NTS 19, 1972–73, 38–64, is sceptical about the presence of the motif of the sacrificial death of martyrs in first-century Palestine.

35. R. T. France, 'The Servant of the Lord in the Teaching of Jesus', Tyn.B 19, 1968, 26–52; *cf.* H. Schürmann, *Der Einsetzungsbericht*, 20–3.

36. J. Jeremias, *The Eucharistic Words of Jesus*, 237–55; G. Wainwright, *Eucharist and Eschatology*, London, 1978, 64–8.

37. Jeremias's exegesis of 1 Cor. 11:26 has been confirmed by O. Hofius, '"Bis dass er kommt" I Kor. XI. 26', NTS 14, 1967–68, 439–41.

38. D. Jones, 'ἀνάμνησις in the LXX and the Interpretation of 1 Cor. XI. 25', JTS 6, 1955, 183–91; A. R. Millard, 'Covenant and Communion in First Corinthians', in W. W. Gasque and R. P. Martin, *Apostolic History and the Gospel*, Exeter, 1970, 242–8.

39. See the discussion of 'Remember, Remembrance' by K. H. Bartels and C. Brown, NIDNTT III, 230–47; B. S. Childs, *Memory and Tradition in Israel*, London, 1962.

40. See above, 47 and n. 67.

41. See above, 44–51.

42. R. Pesch, *Das Abendmahl und Jesu Todesverständnis*, 95f. See *ibid.*, 72–6, for a criticism of attempts to dismember Mk. 14:24 and discover an original, simpler form of the saying.

43. For a convenient summary see D. J. McCarthy, *Old Testament Covenant: A Survey of Current Opinions*, Oxford, 1972.

44. See the unpublished Aberdeen thesis of R. S. Rayburn, 'The contrast between the old and the new covenants in the New Testament' (Ph.D, 1978).

45. I. H. Marshall, *I believe in the historical Jesus*, London, 1977; B. F. Meyer, *The Aims of Jesus*, London, 1979; R. T. France and D. Wenham (ed.), *Gospel Perspectives: Studies of History and Tradition in the Four Gospels*, Vol. 1, Sheffield, 1980.

46. See above, 89; R. Pesch, *op. cit.*, 103–11; B. F. Meyer, *op. cit.*, 216–19.

47. See above, 52.

48. N. Perrin, *Jesus and the Language of the Kingdom*, Philadelphia, 1976; B. D. Chilton, *God in Strength*, Freistadt, 1979.

49. E. Percy, *Die Botschaft Jesus*, Lund, 1953.

50. O. Hofius, *Jesu Tischgemeinschaft mit den Sündern*, Stuttgart, 1967; J. Jeremias, *New Testament Theology*, Vol. 1, London, 1971, 114–16.

51. H. Patsch, 'Abendmahlsterminologie ausserhalb der Einsetzungsberichte', ZNW 62, 1971, 210–31.

52. *Cf.* I. H. Marshall, *The Gospel of Luke*, 357–63.

53. I. H. Marshall, 'The Development of the Concept of Redemption in the New Testament', in R. J. Banks (ed.), *Reconciliation and Hope*, Exeter, 1974, 166f. With reference to Mk. 10:45; 14:24 G. Delling, TRE I, 50, states: 'Substitution here means nothing less than the taking over of the death to which the "many" are all liable through their guilt before God.'
54. H. Patsch, *Abendmahl und historischer Jesus*, 185–97; J. Jeremias, *New Testament Theology* I, 276–81; L. Goppelt, *Theologie des Neuen Testaments* I, 234–41.
55. J. Jeremias, *op. cit.*, I, 292–4; H. Patsch, *op. cit.*, 170–80; L. Goppelt, *op. cit.*, I, 241–7; S. H. T. Page, 'The Authenticity of the Ransom Logion (Mark 10:45b)', in R. T. France and D. Wenham, *op. cit.*, 137–61. The authenticity is denied by R. Pesch, *Das Markusevangelium*, II, 162–4. It is not clear whether J. Roloff, *op. cit.*, (see n. 34) regards Mk. 10:45b as authentic teaching of Jesus or not (apparently the latter, *ibid.*, 54, 63).
56. H. B. Green, *The Gospel according to Matthew*, Oxford, 1975, 212.
57. For liturgical influences on Matthew's treatment of the text see H. Patsch, *op. cit.*, 69f.; J. Jeremias, *The Eucharistic Words of Jesus*, 113f. The view that the changes simply show Matthaean redactional style is upheld by H. Schürmann, *Der Einsetzungsbericht*, 2–7; R. Pesch, *Das Abendmahl und Jesu Todesverständnis*, 24f. Schürmann holds that Matthew's tendency to change narrative statements in Mark into direct speech is visible here. Matthew's alteration makes it clear that in his view the cup-saying preceded the act of drinking by the disciples.
58. H. Patsch, *op. cit.*, 103f., holds that the addition reflects liturgical usage in Matthew's church, since the phrase was one current in the early church and not distinctively Matthaean.
59. There are other small changes in wording in Matthew's account, but none of them are of decisive theological significance.
60. For representatives of this general type of approach see A. Vööbus, 'A New Approach to the Problem of the Shorter and the Longer Text in Luke', NTS 15, 1968–69, 457–463; *id.*, 'Kritische Beobachtungen über die lukanische Darstellung des Herrenmahls', ZNW 61, 1970, 102–110; M. Rese, 'Zur Problematik von Kurz-und Langtext in Luk. XXII. 17ff.', NTS 22, 1975–76, 15–31; R. Pesch, *op. cit.*, 26–34.
61. H. Schürmann, *Jesu Abschiedsrede*, Münster, 1957, 64–99; H. Patsch, *op. cit.*, 170–180; J. Ernst, *Das Evangelium nach Lukas*, 592f.
62. See above, 36–8.
63. I. H. Marshall, *Luke – Historian and Theologian*, Exeter, 1979², 169–75.
64. H. Schürmann, *Der Abschiedsrede*.
65. See especially H. Schürmann, 'Der Abendmahlsbericht Lk 22, 7–38 als Gottesdienstordnung, Gemeindeordnung, Lebensordnung', in *Ursprung und Gestalt*, 108–50, for a non-technical exposition of the whole Lucan narrative, incorporating the insights of his technical studies.
66. See above, 63.
67. I. H. Marshall, *The Gospel of Luke*, 813f.
68. H. Schürmann, *op. cit.*, 139.
69. For this saying *cf.* Matthew 19:28. The relationship between the sayings poses difficult problems; for discussion see I. H. Marshall, *op. cit.*, 814–18.
70. E. Käsemann, *Jesus Means Freedom*, London, 1969, 122–5.

CHAPTER FIVE (pages 107–140)

1. In addition to the commentaries on 1 Corinthians see especially P. Neuenzeit, *Das Herrenmahl: Studien zur paulinischen Eucharistieauffassung*; E. Käsemann, *Essays on New Testament Themes*, London, 1964, 108–35; G. Bornkamm, *Early Christian Experience*, 123–60; G. Delling, *Studien zum Neuen Testament und zum hellenistischen Judentum*, Göttingen, 1970, 318–35; R. Pesch, *Das Abendmahl und Jesu Todesverständnis*, 53–69.

2. Paul, however, does not say that the money is to be collected in the church meeting, but rather that each member is to set aside his contribution on that day and save it up for the common fund.

3. G. Theissen, 'Soziale Integration und sakramentales Handeln. Eine Analyse von 1 Cor. XI. 17–34', Nov.T 16, 1974, 179–206. Several of Theissen's points were already made by earlier writers, but he provides a comprehensive treatment and adduces important background material.

4. Theissen's argument that the breaking of bread and the drinking of the cup were separated by the length of the meal is not convincing. Nor is his view that the rich thought that they had to share only bread and wine justified by the fact that only these items were mentioned in the words of institution.

5. Jude speaks of the 'love-feast', *agapē*. 2 Peter uses the word for 'pleasure' or 'dissipation', *apatē*; the general similarity of language in the two passages suggests that a deliberate play on words is intended. Later scribes assimilated the wording of the two verses.

6. It is unlikely that we are to see allusions to the love feast in Ign. Rom. 7:3; Smyr. 7:1. Other early references to the love feast will be found in Epist. Apost. 15; Tert., Apol. 39; Min. Felix, Oct. 31; Hipp., Apos. Trad. 26.

7. For the separation of Agape and Lord's Supper see Pliny, Ep. 10:96.

8. See above, 41 n. 40.

9. See H. Schürmann, *Der Einsetzungsbericht*, 142–50.

10. *Cf.* P. Neuenzeit, *op. cit.*, 127–54. Neuenzeit appears to us to turn a simple matter into a complicated one by linking the proclamation with the 'remembering', and seeing the death of Jesus as somehow 'present' in the Supper through the presence of the Lord who died in the congregation. This goes well beyond what Paul says in v. 26 and seems quite unnecessary.

11. See the discussion of possible interpretations of the phrase in C. K. Barrett, *The First Epistle to the Corinthians*, 273–5. For the view that the church is meant see W. G. Kümmel in H. Lietzmann and W. G. Kümmel, *An die Korinther I. II.*, Tübingen, 1949, 186; G. Bornkamm, *Early Christian Experience*, 149.

12. *Cf.* P. Neuenzeit, *op. cit.*, 175–83, who speaks of the new identity of the bread and the body of Christ (179), and E. Stauffer, *New Testament Theology*, 163: 'Paul writes of the real and spiritual presence of Christ in the bread and wine'.

13. It is important, however, that Jesus is represented as expressly denying that any and every sickness can be regarded as a penalty for a particular sin.

14. Paul's belief in supernatural acts of judgment hangs together with his belief in supernatural acts of healing and other miraculous signs associated with salvation. Further, Paul could probably claim prophetic powers to discern that a specific event was an act of judgment, but it would be

foolhardy for modern Christians to claim similar prophetic powers. None of the commentators I have consulted really discusses the problem caused by this gap between first-century and twentieth-century beliefs.

15. C. K. Barrett, *op. cit.*, 396–9; G. Bornkamm, *op. cit.*, 169–76.
16. O. Cullmann, *The Christology of the New Testament*, London, 1959, 211ff., thinks that the prayer is for the Lord's coming both at the Supper and at the parousia. Against the association of these passages with the Lord's Supper see G. Delling, *Studien zum Neuen Testament*, 334.
17. H. Schürmann, 'Die Anfänge christlicher Osterfeier' and 'Vorgang und Sinngehalt der urchristlichen Osterfeier', in *Ursprung und Gestalt*, 199–206, 207–9. Schürmann states that 1 Cor. 5:7f. on its own cannot demonstrate whether or not Paul knew of a Christian Passover festival.
18. See L. Goppelt, TDNT VI, 146f.; E. Schweizer, *ibid.*, 437. E. Käsemann, *op. cit.*, 113f., argues that the bread and wine convey *pneuma*. This is quite unconvincing.
19. L. Goppelt, *Theologie des Neuen Testaments*, II, 476f.
20. Some have seen such a rite in Luke 22:17–19a (shorter text) and Didache 9.
21. E. Käsemann, *op. cit.*, 110.
22. L. Goppelt, *op. cit.*, 477f. (*cf. Apostolic and Post-Apostolic Times*, London, 1970, 219) argues that the blessing consecrates the elements, but fails to see that his argument would render *all* food consecrated. Misunderstanding is also present in H. W. Beyer, TDNT II, 763. When Paul says 'which we bless', the emphasis is on 'we Christians' as opposed to the Jews (L. Goppelt, TDNT VI, 156).
23. C. K. Barrett, *op. cit.*, 232, citing H. Lietzmann and W. G. Kümmel, *op. cit.*, 182.
24. F. Hauck, TDNT III, 805; *cf.* H. Seesemann, *Der Begriff κοινωνία im Neuen Testament*, Giessen, 1933, for the same view. The use of *metechō* in v. 17 speaks against this view.
25. L. S. Thornton, *The Common Life in the Body of Christ*, London, 1941, 298; J. A. T. Robinson, *The Body: A Study in Pauline Theology*, London, 1952, 51.
26. E. Best, *One Body in Christ*, London, 1955, 88.
27. C. K. Barrett, *op. cit.*, 234f.
28. F. Hauck, *ibid.*
29. C. K. Barrett, *op. cit.*, 235.
30. S. Aalen, 'Das Abendmahl als Opfermahl im Neuen Testament', Nov. T 6, 1963, 128–52.
31. There is some tension with Acts 17:23, where Paul regards the 'unknown god' as the Christian God worshipped as unknown, and with Acts 17:28 where Paul applies language originally used of Zeus to God. There is a difference, however, between leading men from worship of an unknown god to a true understanding of God and recognising that demonic forces can twist and pervert religion in the form of idolatry.
32. *Cf.* the traditional Roman Catholic understanding of the Supper as a re-presentation of the sacrifice of Jesus. R. Kugelman comments on this passage: 'The parallelism that Paul draws between Jewish and pagan participation in their sacrifices through eating the meat of the victims and Christian fellowship with Christ through the Eucharist shows that he considers the eating of the Eucharist a sacrificial repast and implies that

the Eucharist itself is a sacrifice' (*The Jerome Bible Commentary*, London, 1968, II, 269). Paul 'implies' nothing of the sort.

33. See especially J. Wanke, *Beobachtungen zum Eucharistieverständnis des Lukas.*
34. *Ibid.*, 45.
35. It has been argued that the Emmaus story is meant to recall the meals held by Jesus in Galilee rather than the Last Supper, since the two disciples would not have been present at the latter. However, the important question is what Luke intended his *readers* to make of the story, and there can be little doubt that they were meant to read the story in the light of the Last Supper.
36. M. Wilcox, *The Semitisms of Acts*, Oxford, 1965, 106–9.
37. John 21 is not dependent on Luke but rests on independent tradition.
38. J. Wanke, *op. cit.*, 11–13.
39. J. Jeremias, *The Eucharistic Words of Jesus*, 118–21.
40. *Ibid.*, 120. Whether or not this interpretation be accepted, there would appear to be a clear reference to common meals in Acts 2:46.
41. Since they believed that the Messiah had come, the early Christians would feel all the more justified in worshipping God at the temple and thus expressing their relationship with him in the approved manner. It took some time for them to realise that the death of Jesus had made sacrificial worship obsolete.
42. O. Cullmann, *Early Christian Worship*, London, 1953; O. Cullmann and F. J. Leenhardt, *Essays on the Lord's Supper*, London, 1958. See below, 131.
43. J. Wanke, *op. cit.*, 11–30.
44. This was probably on Sunday evening. See F. F. Bruce, *The Book of the Acts*, London, 1954, 408 n. 25.
45. E. Haenchen, *The Acts of the Apostles*, Oxford, 1971, 586. J. Wanke, *op. cit.*, 23 n. 59, prefers the view that the congregation held their common meal before Paul's sermon, so that the sermon immediately preceded the breaking of bread. This is an attractive view, but v. 11 suggests that the congregation ate after Paul's sermon; perhaps, even if they had eaten before it, they needed some further sustenance after it in view of its inordinate length!
46. J. Wanke, *op. cit.*, 28–30. Cf. J. Jeremias, *op. cit.*, 133.
47. H. Lietzmann, *Mass and Lord's Supper*, 204–15. Similarly, R. Bultmann, *Theology of the New Testament*, London, 1952, I, 57f. For further development along the same lines see W. Marxsen, *The Lord's Supper as a Christological Problem*, with the useful summary of the earlier discussion in the Introduction by J. Reumann.
48. E. Lohmeyer, *Galiläa und Jerusalem*, Göttingen, 1936; 'Das Abendmahl in der Urgemeinde', JBL 56, 1937, 217–52.
49. See n. 42 above.
50. R. Feneberg, *Christliche Passafeier und Abendmahl*, München, 1971.
51. See especially A. J. B. Higgins, *The Lord's Supper in the New Testament*, 56–63; E. Schweizer, *The Lord's Supper according to the New Testament*, 23–8.
52. B. Reicke, *Diakonie, Festfreude und Zelos*, Uppsala, 1951, 141–7; cited by E. Schweizer, *op. cit.*, 24.
53. A somewhat different type of approach is concerned with the suggestion that the accounts of the Last Supper themselves may contain different

strata. See above, 55f., for Schürmann's view that an original account of Jesus' Passover meal with his disciples has been extended by the 'eucharistic account' in Luke 22:19f. The former contains the eschatological perspective, while the latter contains the memorial element. It could be argued that the former was the more primitive account, which was extended by the creation of the words of institution in the early church. However, the basis for this theory is very dubious. See further E. Schweizer, *op. cit.*, 25–8, who considers that the Pauline type of account is 'more or less genuine'.

Yet another view is offered by K. G. Kuhn, 'The Lord's Supper and the Communal Meal at Qumran' (see above, 26 n. 26). He holds that the original cult formula preserved in Mk. 14:22–24 gives us the early church's interpretation of the Last Supper as an Essene cultic meal with bread and wine. The early church celebrated daily meals as a continuation of table-fellowship with Jesus, and these have analogies in the Essene cult-meal. The Marcan formula was then used as a cult formula, as a result of which the accent was switched from eschatological expectation and joy to remembrance of the death of Jesus. The Passover framework of the narrative is later, and is the aetiological cult legend of the Passover fasting of the Jerusalem church. This theory has been sufficiently answered by J. Jeremias, *op. cit.*, 31–6.

54. J. Jeremias, *op. cit.*, 125–37.
55. R. Bultmann, *Das Evangelium des Johannes*, Göttingen, 1959[16], 174–7; E. Lohse, 'Wort und Sakrament im Johannesevangelium', NTS 7, 1960–61, 101–25.
56. The phrase is omitted by a number of western authorities for the text, including, however, only two Greek MSS (D 086). Many commentators regard the words as a scribal insertion, and point to the use of 'the Lord' as a designation of Jesus before the resurrection as an un-Johannine feature (see, however, 11:2; 4:1 *v.l.*).
57. R. Bultmann, *ibid.*; S. Schulz, *Untersuchungen zum Menschensohn-Christologie im Johannes-evangelium*, Göttingen, 1957, 115f. R. E. Brown, *The Gospel according to John*, London, 1971, I, 285–91, holds that the section is Johannine; it is a variant form of the discourse on the bread of life stemming from a different stage in the history of the Johannine preaching.
58. See the balanced discussion in R. Schnackenburg, *Das Johannesevangelium*, Freiburg, 1971, II, 85–9; Schnackenburg himself cautiously favours the view that the chapter is a unity (*ibid.*, 96). See further J. D. G. Dunn, 'John VI – a Eucharistic Discourse?', NTS 17, 1970–71, 328–38.
59. H. Schürmann, 'Jo 6,51c – ein Schlüssel zur grossen johanneischen Brotrede', in *Ursprung und Gestalt*, 151–66.
60. For the variety of interpretations of the passage see R. E. Brown, *op. cit.*, I, 272–4. See further H. Schürmann, 'Die Eucharistie als Repräsentation und Applikation des Heilsgeschehens nach Jo 6,53–58', in *Ursprung und Gestalt*, 167–87. The view presented above is close to that of J. D. G. Dunn, *op. cit.*, who argues that John was dealing with an orthodox reaction to Docetism, as a result of which a literalistic interpretation of the Lord's Supper and an over-emphasis on the physical action had arisen: hence John expounded the view that Jesus himself is the source of eternal life and played down the importance of the sacrament.
61. R. E. Brown, *op. cit.*, I, 109f., lists the points in favour of this view but

must admit that a eucharistic interpretation is nothing more than a possibility. R. Schnackenburg, *op. cit.*, I, 342, is more sceptical. *Cf.* B. Lindars, *The Gospel of John*, London, 1972, 125.

62. According to B. Lindars, *op. cit.*, 487, 'most editors are prepared to admit that the allegory has some connection with the Eucharist', and he himself thinks that the eucharistic benediction over the wine accounts for the imagery. For the view adopted here see L. Morris, *The Gospel according to John*, 668 n. 1; B. F. Westcott, *The Gospel according to St John*, London, 1882, 216f.

63. The order of blood and water surely rules out a reference to baptism and the Lord's Supper, and the view that 'blood' can mean the Lord's Supper is unsubstantiated; see B. Lindars, *op. cit.*, 586f.; L. Morris, *op. cit.*, 819.

64. Ign., Eph. 20:2.

65. S. S. Smalley, *John – Evangelist and Interpreter*, Exeter, 1978, 204–10.

66. We do not consider 1 John 5:8 to be primarily a reference to the Lord's Supper. The water and the blood are the historical water and blood of Jesus' baptism and death, perhaps as these are symbolised in the water of Christian baptism and the wine of the Lord's Supper, but this secondary reference is dubious; see I. H. Marshall, *The Epistles of John*, Grand Rapids, 1978, 238f.

67. Some commentators hold that the thought is purely future and refers to the promise of participation in the heavenly banquet (H. B. Swete, *The Apocalypse of St. John*, London, 1909³, 63f.), but most recent commentators find a reference to present communion with Jesus. While G. B. Caird holds that John is using 'language resonant with eucharistic associations to describe a coming of the Lord even more intimate and personal than that experienced in the corporate worship of the church' (*The Revelation of St John the Divine*, London, 1966, 58), G. R. Beasley-Murray holds that the reminiscences of the Lord's Supper are due rather to allusions to the event to which the Supper itself looks forward (*The Book of Revelation*, London, 1974, 107).

68. For a summary and assessment of the discussion of these passages (Heb. 2:4; 6:4f.; 9:1–14, 20; 10:19f.) see R. Williamson, 'The Eucharist and the Epistle to the Hebrews', NTS 21, 1974–75, 300–12. It is surprising that 10:29 is omitted from consideration; the reference to 'blood' may well reflect the Lord's Supper.

69. O. Michel, *Der Brief an die Hebräer*, Göttingen, 1960¹¹, 342f.

70. This is a commonly held view. P. E. Hughes, *A Commentary on the Epistle to the Hebrews*, Grand Rapids, 1977, 578, cites numerous scholars in support of it including J. Calvin, B. F. Westcott and C. Spicq.

71. S. Aalen, 'Das Abendmahl als Opfermahl im Neuen Testament', Nov.T 6, 1963, 128–52.

72. A. S. Peake, *Hebrews*, Edinburgh, n.d., 241; R. Williamson, *op. cit.*, 308.

73. J. Moffatt, *The Epistle to the Hebrews*, Edinburgh, 1924, 234; R. Williamson, *op. cit.*, 309–12.

74. F. F. Bruce, *The Epistle to the Hebrews*, London, 1964, 401f.

CHAPTER SIX (pages 141–157)

1. L. Goppelt, *Apostolic and Post-Apostolic Times*, 211f., rightly argues that the churches met both for meals and for meetings for teaching and prayer.

2. L. Goppelt, *op. cit.*, 214–21.
3. G. Wainwright, *Eucharist and Eschatology*, London, 1971.
4. See especially F. Hahn, 'Die alttestamentliche Motive in der urchristlichen Abendmahlsüberlieferung', Ev.T 27, 1967, 337–74.
5. E. Lohse, *Märtyrer und Gottesknecht*; D. Hill, *Greek Words and Hebrew Meanings*, Cambridge, 1967.
6. J. Jeremias, TDNT VI, 536–45, especially 541.
7. See, for example, the outline of the historical development in W. Barclay, *The Lord's Supper*.
8. E. Schweizer, *The Lord's Supper according to the New Testament*, 37.

TABLE 1
The Feast of The Passover

Nisan 14: Day of Preparation

Evening:
Morning:
Afternoon: Ritual slaughter of the paschal lamb.
            Preparations for the meal.

Nisan 15: Passover; First Day of Unleavened Bread (Festival 'Sabbath')

Evening: The Passover Meal
 1. Preliminary Course:
    Blessing of festival day (Kiddush) spoken over
    First Cup of wine.
    Dish of green herbs, bitter herbs and fruit sauce.
    Serving of meal and mixing of second cup of wine.

 2. Passover Liturgy:
    The Passover narrative (*haggadah*)
    Singing of Psalm 113 (the little *hallel*)
    Second cup of wine.

 3. Main Meal:
    Grace spoken over bread
    Meal of lamb, unleavened bread, bitter herbs.
    Grace spoken over
    Third cup of wine (cup of blessing).

 4. Conclusion:
    Singing of Psalms 114–118 (the great *hallel*)
    Grace spoken over
    Fourth cup of wine.

Night: Watching and remembrance.

Nisan 16: Second Day of Unleavened Bread (Consecration of first fruits)

Nisan 21: Final Day of Unleavened Bread (Festival 'Sabbath').

TABLE 2

A Synopsis of the Accounts of the Last Supper

Mt. 26:26–29.	Mark 14:22–25.	Luke 22:15–20.	1 Cor. 11:23–25.
		15 And he said to them, 'I have earnestly desired to eat this passover with you before I suffer; 16 for I tell you I shall not eat it until it is fulfilled in the kingdom of God.' 17 And he took a cup, and when he had given thanks he said, 'Take this, and divide it among yourselves; 18 for I tell you that from now on I shall not drink of the fruit of the vine until the kingdom of God comes.	
			23 The Lord Jesus on the night when he was betrayed took bread, 24 and gave thanks, broke it and said,
26 Now as they were eating,	22 And as they were eating,	19 And	
Jesus took bread, and blessed, and broke it, and gave it to the disciples and said, 'Take, eat; this is my body.	he took bread, and blessed, and broke it, and gave it to them, and said, 'Take; this is my body.	he took bread, gave thanks, broke it and gave it to them, saying, 'This is my body which is given for you. Do this in remembrance of me.'	'This is my body which is for you. Do this in remembrance of me.'

TABLE 3

The Development of the Bread-Saying and the Cup-Saying

A. FROM MARK TO LUKE/PAUL

Stage 1	Stage 2	Stage 3
Mark ——————→	Paul ——————→	Luke

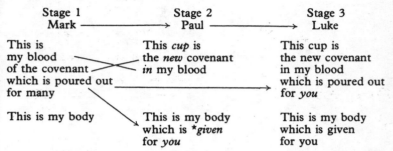

This is
my blood
of the covenant
which is poured out
for many

This is my body

This *cup* is
the *new* covenant
in my blood

This is my body
which is *given*
for *you*

This cup is
the new covenant
in my blood
which is poured out
for *you*

This is my body
which is given
for you

(Stage 2: reformulation of first part of cup-saying, followed by transfer of second part to bread-saying with appropriate changes and substitution of 'you' for 'many'. Stage 3: conflation of Pauline and Marcan forms of cup-saying by Luke.)

B. FROM PAUL TO MARK

Stage 2	Stage 1	Stage 3
Mark ←——————	Paul ——————→	Luke

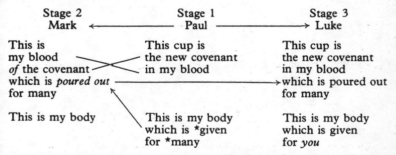

This is
my blood
of the covenant
which is *poured out*
for many

This is my body

This cup is
the new covenant
in my blood

This is my body
which is *given*
for *many*

This cup is
the new covenant
in my blood
which is poured out
for many

This is my body
which is given
for *you*

(Stage 1: The Pauline wording, possibly with the inclusion of 'given' (Luke) and an original 'many'. Stage 2: assimilation of first part of cup-saying to bread-saying, followed by omission of redundant second part of bread-saying. Stage 3: conflation of Pauline and Marcan forms of cup-saying by Luke.)

Mt. 26:26–29.	Mark 14:22–25.	Luke 22:15–20.	1 Cor. 11:23–25.
27 And he took a cup,	23 And he took a cup,	20 And the cup likewise after supper	25 Likewise also the cup after supper,
and when he had given thanks he gave it to them,	and when he had given thanks he gave it to them, and they all drank of it. 24 And he said to them,		
saying, 'Drink of it, all of you:		saying,	saying,
28 for this is my blood of the covenant, which is poured out for many for the forgiveness of sins.	'This is my blood of the covenant, which is poured out for many.	'This cup is the new covenant in my blood, which is poured out for you.	'This cup is the new covenant in my blood.
			Do this, as often as you drink it, in remembrance of me.'
29 I tell you I shall not drink again of this fruit of the vine until that day when I drink it new with you in my Father's kingdom.'	25 Truly, I tell you I shall not drink again of the fruit of the vine until that day when I drink it new in the kingdom of God.'	16 'For I tell you I shall not eat it until it is fulfilled in the kingdom of God.'	18 'For I tell you that from now on I shall not drink of the fruit of the vine until the kingdom of God comes.'

C. FROM LUKE TO MARK AND PAUL

Stage 2a Paul ←	Stage 1 —— Luke ——	Stage 2b → Mark
This cup is the new covenant in my blood	This cup is the new covenant in my blood which is poured out for *many	This is my blood *of* the covenant which is poured out for many
This is my body which is for *you*	This is my body which is given for *many	This is my body

(Stage 1: the Lucan wording with an original 'many'. Stage 2a: omission of the redundant second part of the cup-saying in the Pauline tradition and replacement of 'many' by 'you'. Stage 2b: assimilation of first part of cup-saying to bread-saying in the Marcan tradition, followed by omission of redundant second part of bread-saying.)

In the above diagrams the cup-saying has been placed before the bread-saying for ease of presentation. Only the broad outline of the possible developments is given.

TABLE 4
The Chronology of the Last Supper

	1. Mark and John in disagreement		2. The Pharisees and the Sadducees in disagreement (Billerbeck)		3. The Qumran sect and the official calendar in disagreement (Jaubert)		4. The Galileans and Judaeans in disagreement (Hoehner)	
	Mark	John	Pharisees/Mark	Sadducees/John	Qumran/Jesus	Sadducees/John	Galileans/Mark	Judaeans/John
Tues.	13	12	13	12	15 Supper	12	12	12
Wed.	14	3	14	13	Jewish trial — 16	13	13	13
Thurs.	Sacrifice		Sacrifice		Roman trial		14 Sacrifice	

	15 Passover/Supper · 14 Supper	14 Supper	15 Passover/Supper	14 Supper	17	14	Passover/Supper	14 Supper
Fri.	Trials Cross	Trials Cross/Sacrifice	Trials Cross	Trials Cross/Sacrifice	Cross	Cross Sacrifice	15 Cross	Trials Cross/Sacrifice
	16 · 15 Passover	15 Passover	16	15 Passover	18	15 Passover	16	15 Passover
Sat.	17 · 16	16	17	16	19	16	16	16
Sun.	Empty Tomb	Empty Tomb	Empty Tomb	Empty Tomb	Empty Tomb	Empty Tomb	17 Empty Tomb	Empty Tomb
	18 · 17	17	18	17	20	17		17

------ Midnight
====== Sunset

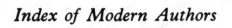

Index of Modern Authors

INDEX OF MODERN AUTHORS